My First Pictorial Encyclopedia

SBN 7063 1206 6

Impreso en los Talleres de EDITORIAL FHER, S. A.
Calle Villabaso, 9.– BILBAO-ESPAÑA

PRINTED IN SPAIN

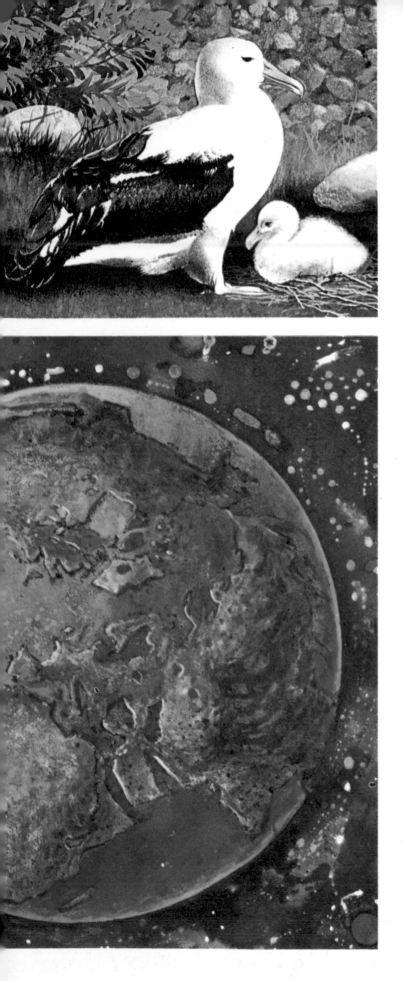

My First Pictorial Encyclopedia

Edited and compiled by
J. L. Courtney and
G. E. Speck

Ward Lock & Co. Limited
London and Sydney

Aeroplanes

Ever since earliest times, men have wanted to fly. One of the oldest accounts of man's dream of flying is in the Greek legend of how Daedalus and his son, Icarus, made wings of wax and feathers to escape from Minos, the King of Crete. Flying high in the sky with his bird-like wings, Icarus ignored his father's advice and flew too near the sun, which melted the wax in his wings and sent him plunging to his death.

One of the first great thinkers to turn his mind to the problem of flight was the Greek philosopher Aristotle (384—322 B.C.).

However, his theories about how things fly were not correct, and besides, he never made any practical tests to try out his ideas.

The man who gave real thought to the subject of flight was the Italian genius, Leonardo da Vinci (1452—1519). He designed a machine with flapping wings but it was never built and tested. Leonardo also experimented with the "Chinese top"; today this is a toy propeller which is launched by being pushed up a spiral shaft.

Many of the most important and practical advances in flying were made three hundred years later by the "father of flying", Sir George Cayley (1773—1857). Cayley made a number of gliders, and if he had had the right sort of engine his gliders would certainly have flown. Unfortunately Cayley's ideas were not given the support they de-

Modern airports such as Orly Airport, Paris, are well-equipped for the smooth arrival and departure of the planes and the safety and comfort of the passengers.

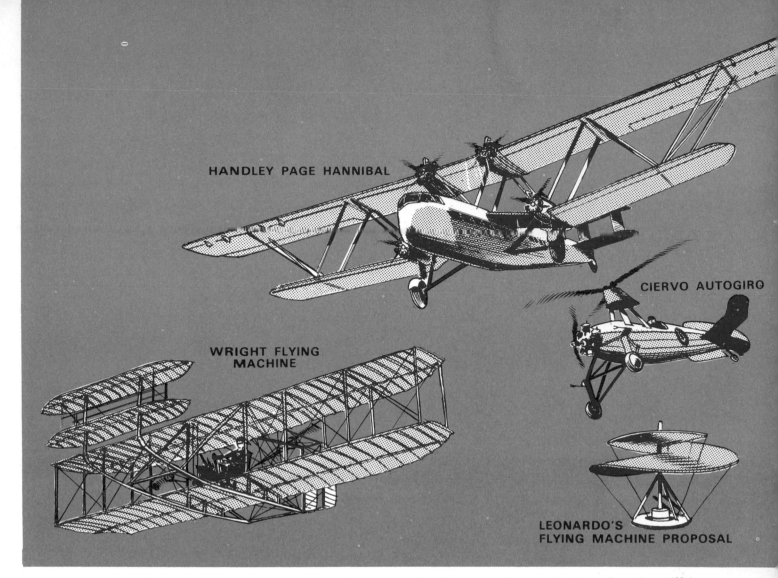

HANDLEY PAGE HANNIBAL

CIERVO AUTOGIRO

WRIGHT FLYING MACHINE

LEONARDO'S FLYING MACHINE PROPOSAL

served, mainly because at the time people were more interested in the balloon, which had recently been invented and which was thought to be the most likely means of flight.

One of the first power-driven aeroplanes was designed by William Henson (1805—88) and John Stringfield (1799—1883). Henson built a large model of the machine, which was driven by a steam engine. However, it did not do what was expected of it and the idea was abandoned. At about the same time, much work was being done on flying machines in Europe, some of the most important of which was done by the Lilienthal brothers. They designed and built a number of gliders and were the first to use a curved wing——a form of wing that is still in use. It was while flying one of his gliders that one of the brothers, Otto, crashed to his death.

The first men to fly an engine-propelled aeroplane were the Americans, Wilbur and Orville Wright. These brothers were very interested in the work of the Lilienthal brothers and made several gliders following the Lilienthals' ideas. In 1902, when the Wright brothers had designed and built a successful glider, they turned their attentions to powered flight. They built their own petrol engine and made their aircraft ready to fly from Kill Devil Hill, Kitty Hawk, North Carolina, on December 17,

1903. Orville made the first flight of 12 seconds at a speed of 30—35 m.p.h. Three more flights were made that day, the last covering a distance of 852 feet and lasting 59 seconds. In 1905 they made a circular flight of $24\frac{1}{4}$ miles in 38 minutes, 3 seconds, in Dayton, Ohio. The Wright brothers were granted a patent for their flying machine in 1906.

Although the flights of the Wright brothers did not claim the attention they deserved, they did prove that man could fly in a power-driven machine, and this inspired other pioneers of flight to carry on.

Aeroplanes fly by the same principle that keeps birds airborne. When an aeroplane moves forward, the air flows over and under the wings, and because of their special shape and the angle at which they meet the airstream a powerful upward force is produced. This force is known as "lift" and is made up of two parts: 1, that caused by the air pushing up on the underside of the wing, and 2, the suction above the wing which pulls the wing up with a force twice as strong as the force pushing from below.

Briefly, the main parts of an aeroplane are the wings, which support the weight of the machine; the engine (piston or jet), which supplies the power to move the aeroplane forward; the fin and rudder, which control the direction of flight; and the undercarriage, which enables the aircraft to land safely. Slots increase lift at take-off, and wing flaps on the aircraft act as brakes when the plane is landing.

Until about ten years ago most aircraft were powered by the ordinary piston-type engine. Since then, an increasing number of long-distance and high-speed aeroplanes have been powered by turboprops and jet engines. This does not mean, however, that the piston-type is no longer of any value or no longer to be seen at airports. It is still

In the cockpit of the modern airliner are panels covered with dials, buttons and switches—all of which are important to the running and safety of the plane.

Airliners like this one and the "Concorde" will soon make the traveller's journey across the Atlantic a matter of two or three flying hours.

used in many types of aircraft, especially those used for carrying freight.

Turboprop engines are powered by special types of jet engines which drive propellers. They are not as fast as the pure jets, but they have advantages which make them excellent airliners on many routes. Turboprops can be used either to fly as far as the jets or to fly short distances, landing at many points along the route to drop off and pick up passengers. Turboprops are, in addition, the quietest of the large modern airliners.

The largest and fastest airliners are powered by jets, and they travel the farthest distances. If you watch a jet airliner taking off you will notice how steeply it climbs away from the runway and how quickly it vanishes high up in the sky. Jet airliners usually fly at a height of about eight or nine miles. At these heights they leave behind them white vapour trails.

Because of the ever-increasing use of aeroplanes for travel and transport, airports have grown larger and larger so that the biggest ones now cover enormous areas with airline buildings, aeroplane hangars, and runways. Even the busiest airport manages to keep track of all the planes that are constantly taking off and landing so that terrible accidents do not occur. The coming and going of airliners at an airport is directed from the control tower. In the top room, busy controllers use radio and other aids to make sure that airliners take off and land at the correct times and on the right runways. The men in the tower can talk to the pilot of each plane as it is arriving and give him the proper directions for landing. In the lower room are the men who control all the movements of aircraft on the ground. By radio and telephone they are in touch with the aircraft on the ground, also with ground staff whose job it is to guide the airliners as they taxi in. The control tower is the heart of the airport.

Africa

The continent of Africa, which stretches north-south from the Mediterranean Sea to the Cape of Good Hope in the South Atlantic, covers a vast area and includes a variety of climates and peoples.

Stretching across the northern part of Africa is the great Sahara Desert. Formerly the desert was inhabited only by those who lived in the scattered oases and cultivated grain crops, dates and fruit; and by the nomads who moved with their tents and camels as the seasons changed. Now that oil, natural gas and iron ore are being taken out of the desert the pattern of life in the Sahara is changing. New towns are springing up in the heart of the desert to supply the needs of oil men. Air-conditioned homes and shops have been built, power and water laid on, and facilities provided for contact with the outside world—roads and airfields.

Along the western coast of Africa the climate is what is known as "equatorial", because it is quite close to the equator. Countries like Nigeria, Ghana and the Ivory Coast have two seasons, wet and dry, and the temperature is high all the year round. The rainy season lasts from April to October and the dry season from November to March. As one moves from the coastal to the inland areas, the landscape changes quite sharply. The low, swampy strip along

Mount Kilimanjaro in Tanzania is the highest mountain in Africa. Its highest peaks, covered in snow, are 19,500 feet in altitude.

The Victoria Falls, in Rhodesia, were discovered by David Livingstone in 1855, and are today a great tourist attraction.

the Atlantic Ocean gives way to tropical rain forests, savannah grasslands, woodlands, and finally to mountains on a high plateau. Agriculture is one of the main sources of wealth to the nations of West Africa, for many crops important to the rest of the world are grown here: coffee, cocoa, cotton, oil-palms, soya beans and ground-nuts are perhaps the most common.

Africa's two most important rivers are the Nile and the Congo. The Nile flows north from its source in Lake Victoria to the Mediterranean. Egypt, or the United Arab Republic, is in the north-east of Africa and depends entirely on the Nile for its water. The Congo River, in central Africa, flows westward through the dense tropical jungles of the Congo Republic, emptying into the Atlantic Ocean. This central sec-

tion of the continent is a land of striking contrasts. Geographically it is part tropical forest and part savannah land. The forests produce very little other than small quantities of wild rubber and elephant ivory. It has been, and still is, the natural home of such rare, shy creatures as the gorilla and okapi, the cousin of the giraffe. The forest is also the home of the pygmy, whose life is still not very different from that of the food hunters of prehistoric times. In the Congo Republic there are rich deposits of minerals, including copper, diamonds and radium.

To the east of the Congo valley is the mountainous area of the Central African plateau, from which rises Mount Kilimanjaro. At 19,500 feet it is the highest mountain in Africa. Most of the newly-formed

The Fulanis are a tribe of nomadic herdsmen who live in an area stretching from Senegal in the west to the Chad in the east. Above: *A Fulani watches his cattle.* Right: *West African women and children in a Nigerian village.*

states in East Africa, such as Kenya and Tanzania, are concerned with building up their agricultural production and setting up light industry. Kenya's main crop is coffee, but other crops such as tea and cotton are also grown. The Nairobi National Park, a game reserve, is near the capital of Kenya. On it can be seen a wonderful range of Africa's wild-life—lions, rhinoceroses, elephants, giraffes, zebras and many kinds of antelope. The main commercial crops of most of these countries are cotton, coffee, oil seeds and sisal, and all of these are exported in great quantities.

The largest lake in Africa, Lake Victoria, is in East Africa. Among the fresh-water lakes of the world it ranks second in size, Lake Superior in the United States being the largest. Lake Victoria covers an area of 26,000 square miles, and is the main reservoir for the Nile River. It lies within the borders of three countries—Tanzania, Kenya and Uganda.

If you look on the map you can see that South Africa is a very large country. It occupies most of the area at the southern end of the continent and includes many mountains and rivers within its boundaries. There are the southern ranges around the Table Mountain and the great range of the Drakensbergs in the east of the country. The high land in the centre is excellent grazing land, and there, too, are the richest farmlands and mineral resources anywhere in Africa. In the south are a series of mountain ranges rising to a wide plateau and to the north are more fertile plains for pasture. Natal in the east is the most fertile land of all, running along the coastline.

This region at the southern end of the African continent is tremendously rich in mineral resources. South Africa contains large gold mines producing enormous yearly quantities. There are also diamond, coal, copper and silver mines and tin and asbestos are important. A country with such re-

The Queen Elizabeth Park in Uganda is a large game reserve, where great numbers of wild animals are protected by the government.

sources would be rich without farming land as well, but the produce of South African farms is almost as great as the mineral wealth. All kinds of crops are grown, the most important being wheat, maize, barley, oats and fruits. South Africa also attracts many tourists, who come to admire the natural beauty of the country and to enjoy its large beaches and holiday resorts.

At this point in time, much of the African continent is in a state of dramatic change and growth. Countries which were once ruled by Europeans have only just gained their independence, and as young, newly-formed nations they are struggling to make their place in the modern world. Steps are being taken everywhere to improve education, build up industry and modernize agriculture, and in carrying out these tasks the African states are receiving aid and advice from many of the other nations of the world.

Nigerian women preparing the soil for the next crop. It is normal for women to work in groups on the land. One of the most important crops grown in this area is the groundnut.

11

The American Continent

A herd of alpacas high in the Andes Mountains of Chile.

The American Continent is the large body of land between the Atlantic and the Pacific Oceans that makes up what is called the Western Hemisphere. It is divided into two main parts, North America and South America, joined in the middle by the countries of Central America. The northernmost point in the Americas is the North Pole; from there the continent stretches south as far as Tierra del Fuego, at the tip of South America. Because it was not discovered by Europeans until the late 1400's, the American Continent was called "the New World" after Columbus first set eyes on it in 1492.

The Americas were not "new" to some people, however. Many, many years before Columbus crossed the Atlantic Ocean, early peoples from Siberia and other areas in northern Asia made their way across the Bering Straits into what is now Alaska and moved down into Canada. The ones who stayed in Alaska and northern Canada we know today as Eskimos. Others went further, and became the red Indians of southern Canada and the United States. Over the years still others made their way down into Central and South America. The great cities of the Incas in Peru and the Mayans and Aztecs in Mexico were built up by the children, grand-children and great grand-children of these early wanderers. The ruins of many of these cities, with their enormous stone temples and palaces, can still be seen today.

We may find it hard to believe that a South American Indian and an Eskimo are in any way related. But wherever these early Asian peoples went they had to use the animals and plants that they found for food, clothing, and shelter, and they had to get used to many different climates. Alaska and northern Canada were cold and icy lands, where very few plants and animals could live. The Eskimos who settled there had to learn to build their houses from ice and snow and to take their food from the sea. The ground was either frozen or too rocky for farming. The Indians who settled in the Amazon River Valley in South America, on the other hand, found themselves in a hot, tropical land overgrown with dense jungle. They needed less clothing and since there were lots of animals living in the jungle they hunted their food on land. Their houses had to be cool instead of warm and were built of grass and vines instead of ice. All these things made their lives very different from their brothers in the North, so that today the Eskimos

Indian women of the Andes spinning llama wool to make cloth. Bowler hats are worn by nearly all these highland women.

A view from the air of Rio de Janeiro, showing the magnificent harbour. The peak at top right is the famous Sugar Loaf Mountain.

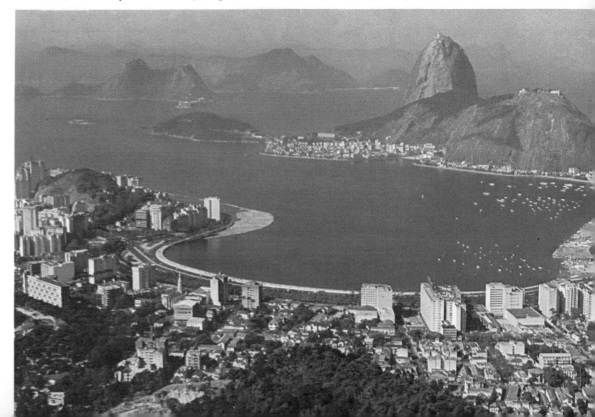

Ultra-modern building block in Brasilia, the new capital of Brazil. The design for the completely modern city was chosen in a competition.

and the Amazon Indians are really two separate peoples. Many of the Indians living in South America live today just as they have lived for hundreds of years.

The frozen North and the tropical rain forest are only two of the many different areas and climates that make up the American Continent. A great chain of mountains runs down from Canada into the United States, where it becomes the American Rockies. The chain carries on through Mexico and Central America and down into South America, into Peru and Bolivia and finally into the great Andes Mountains which run down the length of Chile. All of these mountain areas are rich in minerals such as gold, iron, coal, tin and copper, and today modern methods

of mining take these precious ores out of the earth so that they may be made useful to man.

There are also flat areas, or prairies, on the American Continent that are covered with grass and low shrubs. Very few trees grow on the plains. The Great Plains in the United States and the wide *pampas* in Argentina are examples of grasslands that today are large farming and ranching areas. In fact, the American cowboys herding cattle on the ranges of the Great Plains lead very much the same lives as the *gauchos* of Argentina, who are sometimes called the cowboys of South America. The climate on the plains is generally dry, with very cold winters and very hot summers. These regions often contain large deposits of crude

Aerial view of part of the Brazilian rain forest; forests similar to these cover millions of square miles of central Brazil.

The Grand Canyon, U.S.A., probably the most spectacular canyon in the world. It is some 200 miles long and in places nearly a mile deep. The Colorado River, which formed the canyon, is at bottom right

oil, or petroleum, under the ground. The discovery of oil in parts of Texas and Oklahoma in America has made many people in these states rich, since oil is today one of the most useful raw materials in the world.

The continent even has its own desert—the Great American Desert in North America. Here nature has carved out strange and beautiful landscapes in rock and sand. One of the most famous attractions in the United States is the Grand Canyon, carved out over thousands of years by the waters of the Colorado River which runs through it. The desert is more difficult for man to live in, and for hundreds of years the only people who lived there were Indians, who knew how to find water and how to protect themselves from the heat. Now, however, men have learned how to bring water into dry areas so that people can live comfortably, and in some

A giant saguaro cactus in the arid Arizona desert. The size of the man sitting on the ground shows just how large this cactus is!

New York City, viewed here from the southern end of Manhattan.
Manhattan is an island and was once a Dutch settlement. Today
it has the greatest concentration of skyscrapers anywhere in the world.

Niagara Falls, one of the
great tourist attractions
in North America. There
are two falls, one in
America and the other
in Canada; they are
separated by Goat Island.

The forested Shield country in Canada, which stretches to Hudson Bay. Areas like this produce much lumber for the papermaking industry.

The tropical landscape of Florida in the South-east United States. A warm, sunny climate makes Florida a favourite spot for winter holidays.

Bryce Canyon, Utah, U.S.A. A fairy-tale land of sandstone carved by rain, frost, wind and sun, at sunset it is coloured a lovely soft mixture of reds, pinks, and chromes.

Harvesting on the Great Plains, Colorado, with a team of combine harvesters. This region of the United States is often called the "Breadbasket of the Nation", because it produces so much of the wheat for America and the rest of the world.

areas the soil has been made wet and fertile enough to grow crops.

The eastern and western coastal areas of the United States and Canada have a milder climate because they are near the sea. It is never as hot as tropical South America nor as cold as the Arctic, and never as dry as the American desert nor as wet as the rain forests of Brazil. It is in this more comfortable climate that most people live, and most of the great cities of the United States and Canada are in this area. Many cities have grown up where there are natural harbours. New York, San Francisco, Montreal and Quebec are ports in North America, while in South America Buenos Aires, Rio de Janeiro and Valparaiso are all port cities.

The people that now live in these cities and indeed all over North and South America come from many different lands. After Columbus discovered the New World and its Indian inhabitants, people began to emigrate from many European countries. The Spanish conquered and settled Central and South America; the English, Dutch and French were the first to set up colonies in North America. They came for many reasons. Some, like the American Pilgrims, came to escape being punished for their religious beliefs. Others came to escape famines and hard times at home in the hope of starting a better life in a new land. Some even came as prisoners, for at one time England set up prison colonies in America to hold the overflow from her prisons at home. And many Africans were brought by force to the New World as slaves to work on the large sugar and cotton plantations in the West Indies and the American South.

This was only the beginning. Since the first English settlers landed on Plymouth Rock in America, people of all the European and most of the Asian nations have come to the New World. While South America has remained mostly Spanish and Portuguese, North America has become a great "melting pot" of nationalities.

When the Spanish first came to the New World they were looking for riches. It was the gold and silver belonging to the Indians that they were after, but what they found of that soon ran out. Today, however, we know that the Spanish were right. There were great riches to be found in the New World, but not in gold. North and South America today help to supply the rest of the world with many important and valuable things. Much of the world's cof-fee and cocoa comes from South America, and much of the world's beef from Argentina and the United States. We have already seen that there were vast mineral deposits in the mountains of the Americas, and oil reserves under the plains. Canada and the United States grow enough wheat and corn to supply themselves and many other countries as well. Large industries turn raw materials into products that are need-ed all over the world, and modern methods of transportation make it easy to send these products to countries everywhere. Large networks of railways help to speed these cargoes to the coastal ports, where they are loaded on to ships and planes to be carried overseas. In recent years the St. Lawrence River in Canada has been extended to reach the Great Lakes, and is called the St. Lawrence Seaway. It is now possible for a ship to go from the Altantic Ocean inland to the middle of the North American continent. Detroit, an inland city in the United States is now a a bustling port, though it is over 700 miles from the sea!

The iron and steel plant at Hamilton, South Ontario. From the shores of Lake Ontario the steel is shipped directly to the Atlantic via the St. Lawrence Seaway.

Animals With Pouches and Other Unusual Creatures

The female spiny anteater, native to Australia, carries her young in a pouch until their growing spines become uncomfortable for her.

The kangaroo is probably the most famous of the world's pouched animals, but there are a number of other animals with the same kind of pockets in which they carry their young. Most of these pouched animals, and several more of Nature's most unusual creatures, are natives of Australia.

Animals with pouches are called *marsupials*, from a Latin word meaning "pouch". When their young are born, they climb up through the mother's fur and into the pouch, where they are warm and protected. Most of these animals eat insects or plants; very few are meat-eaters. One of the rarest of the meat-eating type is the Tasmanian wolf. It is a dog-like creature with a long tail and a back marked with black bands. Its natural food is wallabies, rats, and birds, but after the white settlers went to Australia, it started to kill sheep and poultry as well. Farmers began killing off these animals, and now they are known only in Tasmania, where they are rare.

Another meat-eater is the dasyure, or the native cat of Australia, which is much

larger than an ordinary house cat. It, too, has been killed off in great numbers because of its poultry-killing habits, but it has been able to survive better than the Tasmanian wolf because it gives birth to many young at a time. A female native cat may have as many as twenty-four little ones at once!

One animal with a pouch that eats insects and vegetables is the bandicoot, which is about the size of a rabbit but has stiff fur. The long-nosed bandicoot can be a pest in gardens, for it burrows with its nose into the ground in search of insects to eat. The rabbit-bandicoot has long, rabbit-like ears and can burrow as fast as a man can dig.

Two pouched animals that belong to the same family as the bandicoot are the phalangers and the koalas. Both have a thumb-like paw for grasping, and they feed on leaves, fruit, flowers, honey and insects. The flying phalanger, the largest of which, the great glider, is the size of a cat, spends the daytime in holes and trees and comes out at night to make long gliding leaps from tree to tree. These animals have a long fold of skin between their fore- and hind-legs which spreads out like a parachute to keep them in the air. The koala, sometimes called the Australian teddy bear, is small and brown and bear-like, with tufted ears and a beak-like snout. These cuddly-looking little animals are in danger of being wiped out, for they eat only eucalyptus leaves, and many of these trees have been cut down for their gum. Attempts are now being made to save the koalas by setting up parks for them.

The kangaroo is the largest of the pouched animals, and may measure up to ten feet from the tip of its nose to the end of its long tail. Kangaroos have long and very strong hind legs, which they use for jumping. Their front legs are small, and they have powerful tails which they use to help them sit in an upright position when they are resting. Kangaroos range in size from the small rat-kangaroos, which look something like rats but are the size of rabbits; to the tree kangaroos and rock wallabies, two or three feet high; to the great red and grey kangaroos measuring ten feet.

The duckbill platypus, one of Nature's oddest creatures, has webbed feet and a bill like a duck, a flat tail like a beaver, and thick greyish-brown fur like an otter. It lays eggs like a bird, but it is actually a mammal, and the female feeds her young milk.

Australia and New Zealand

Of all the continents in the world, Australia is the smallest, but at the same time it is the world's largest island! It lies in the southern half of the Pacific Ocean, south of Asia but north of the Antarctic Circle. Part of Australia has a tropical climate, with warm winters and hot summers, and much of the continent is desert—dry, with little or no rainfall. This has been a great problem to Australians who want to farm the land, for crops, animals and people need plenty of water to survive. They have therefore devised systems to bring water into dry areas, so that in many places farming is now possible. One of these systems is the Snowy Mountain Scheme in New South Wales. This scheme is one of the largest in the world, so big in fact that although parts of it are already in use, the entire system is not expected to be finished before 1974. It provides not only water for dry areas, but also electric power to run Australia's industries. Valuable minerals such as lead, zinc, iron, copper and bauxite have been discovered in the inland desert regions, so that the land, dry as it is, is still very useful.

Australia became an island very early in geological times, and as a result it is the home of many unusual and interesting animals. Two of the most famous of these are the koala and the kangaroo. Kangaroos are different from other animals in that they raise and protect their young in a pouch. The kangaroo has been made the emblem of Australia.

Considering the large size of the country, there are very few people living there. Most of those who do are English-speaking immigrants. Over ten million more are Europeans and the remainder are Chinese and aborigines. The aborigines were the first to settle in Australia; they had been there for some fifteen thousand years before the Europeans arrived. Until very recently they lived much as they had for thousands of years, but now many have taken to Western ways of living, working as ranch hands on cattle farms. A few tribes still follow a traditional way of life in the Northern Territory.

In the eastern part of Australia a great deal of sheep and dairy farming is done, and the country's main exports are wool, meat and wheat. Although wool is the largest of Australia's exported products,

Steam caused by volcanic activity under the earth is harnessed both for heating homes and for the production of electric power in New Zealand today.

and allows her to buy many necessities from other countries, great increases are are now being made in the production of other crops. Cotton and rice growing has been developing rapidly, and will soon meet the needs of the country so that these products will not have to be imported from outside Australia. The western part of the continent is dry and desert-like, and it is here that a great deal of cattle ranching is done. Along the coast are Australia's great cities, where industries such as the large lead refinery at Port Pirie are growing steadily. The coastal areas also boast the most pleasant climate, and since it is warm and sunny, the coastline is dotted with holiday resorts to which city-dwellers flock

Herding a flock of merino sheep, Australia. The herder, in his wide-brimmed hat and high boots, works on horseback and looks very much like an American cowboy. A sheep farm in Australia is not called a ranch, but a "station."

Ayers Rock near Alice Springs in central Australia. This landscape of desert and scrubby trees is typical of the central and western regions of the continent. The patterns in the sand in the foreground are made by the action of the wind as it sweeps across the flat land.

A typical Australian farm. This one is near Broken Hill in New South Wales. The windmill at left runs a pump that draws water up from the deep well in the ground.

all year round.

More than half the total population of Australia live in the six capital cities of the six Australian states: Sydney, Brisbane, Adelaide, Perth, Melbourne and Hobart. Even though many Australians are town dwellers they spend enough time outdoors to excel in many sports, and especially in cricket and tennis. They have a reputation all over the world for being outstanding sportsmen.

New Zealand is the country to the southeast of Australia, and is made up of a group of islands. The islands range widely in size, but it is on the two largest islands, known as North and South Island, that most of New Zealand's people live.

New Zealand was discovered by Captain Abel Tasman in 1642. Tasman had been sent to explore Australia, but had gone too far southwest of that continent and reached Tasmania and New Zealand instead. The man who did most toward the mapping of Australia and New Zealand was Captain James Cook, who made several charting expeditions about 1770. The Europeans who settled in New Zealand arrived much later than the Maoris, the native Polynesians who had come to New Zealand from Raratongo in the middle 1300's. The Maoris have now come to follow the Western way of life, though they preserve many of the old traditions.

The North Island is mountainous and has the geysers and hot springs for which New Zealand is famous. A geyser is a column of hot water and steam that shoots into the air from a hole in the ground. This usually happens at fairly regular intervals, and is a result of volcanic activity under the earth. The geysers in New Zealand were mostly inactive in 1880, but in 1886 the great Tarawera eruption brought new geysers into existence when water, steam, mud and stones were hurled 600 to 800 feet into the air.

The Southern Island of New Zealand contains the Canterbury plains, which are grazing grounds for the sheep that are raised there. Sheep and wool are New Zealand's largest exports, and there are twenty-six times as many sheep in New Zealand as there are people! Because New Zealand sells so much meat and wool to other countries, the invention of the first refrigerator ship, which could keep cargoes of meat cold, ensured the success of the country's agricultural industry. It was a great moment when, in 1882, the ship *Dunedin* set sail from Wellington with the first cargo of refrigerated meat.

There is not a great deal of mineral production in New Zealand, though gold mining was at one time an important source of wealth. Some of the minerals now mined in small quantities are copper, silver, iron ore, manganese ore, tungsten and asbestos.

Because New Zealand has a population of under two million, there is lots of space and enough jobs for everyone and the standard of living is high. The climate is mild and moist, and changes little during the year so that several crops may be grown during one season. The only heavy snowfalls occur in the New Zealand Alps, which are often used as a training ground for mountain climbing expeditions to the Himalayas.

Birds of the World

Millions of years ago, birds were rather like lizards with feathers. The first bird we know about was nearly the size of a crow and lived in Europe about 150 million years ago. It had a lizard-like snout with a row of tiny teeth along the top and bottom jaws. Its tail was a curious cross between a bird's tail and a lizard's tail, for it was long with many small bones, but feathers grew out of its whole length. It probably did not flap its wings to fly like the birds of today. The wings and tail were used mainly for gliding. This strange creature had two clawed fingers sticking out of the front of each wing and these helped the bird to climb up trees and clamber along the branches in search of food.

Of all the animals, only birds have feathers, but like mammals they are warm-blooded and have backbones. Feathers not only keep birds warm, but also enable them to fly. Most birds' wings consist of long, stiff feathers which, for their weight, are stronger than steel. The large, nearly weightless area of the wings can easily hold the bird up in the air, and the great power needed to flap the wings is supplied by the bird's chest muscles, which are very strong. A bird's tail is used chiefly for keeping the bird on an even keel, but as a bird lands the tail is also used as a brake. It is fanned downwards and slows down the speed of flight. At the same time the bird beats its wings with a forward motion a few times and its speed drops below the point where flying is possible, and so it lands.

The way in which a bird flies is controlled by the shape of its wings. Eagles, for example, have long, broad wings, and can spend long periods soaring and gliding

*The dipper inhabits the banks of rocky streams in Europe
and Northern Asia. It captures fresh-water molluscs
under the water, walking along the bottom of the stream.
Along the bank, it builds a cup-shaped nest in the tall
grasses, in which it lays four to seven white eggs.*

27

on rising currents of air. Occasionally they slowly flap their wings. Swallows and terns, on the other hand, are fast-flying birds that travel great distances. Their wings are long and pointed and produce rapid, continuous flight. Very different is a bird like a pheasant which spends most of its time on the ground and only flies short distances. Its wings are short and rounded and when it flies, it beats its wings rapidly yet covers only a few yards at a time.

Birds use their voices more than any other animal and each bird has its own special call or song. The songs of the thrush and canary are pleasant to listen to, but there are other birds whose voices are not so pleasing to our ears, as anyone will know who has been to a parrot house at a zoo. But whether they are pleasant or not, these calls all have a special meaning. They may be a warning that an enemy is ap-

The albatross breeds on remote islands in the ocean, producing one egg in a season. Both parents incubate the egg and care for the young bird when it hatches.

The penguin, a native of the Antarctic regions, is an awkward creature on land; once in the water, however, it is an excellent swimmer, diver and fisherman.

proaching, a challenge to a rival bird, a signal to young chicks, and many other messages. Most often a song is used by a bird to tell other birds that he has marked out his territory. By "claiming" a territory, a bird makes sure that he has a feeding ground for his family, for if other birds entered it, there would not be food enough to go round.

Bird-song, therefore, has its uses, even when it is that of the lyre bird, probably the most beautiful songster of all. The lyre bird lives in the ferny glades of the forests of south-eastern Australia. The male has a lyre-shaped tail, which it spreads when displaying to the hen. The lyre bird is not content with its own song but will imitate the songs of all other birds it hears, and will also imitate, or mimic, the sounds of cars, tractors, and other mechanical things!

There are about 8,600 different kinds of birds and of these over 5,000 are perching birds. The birds in this large group are varied but are related by possessing a

The male Satin Bower Bird builds a "bower" of small twigs in his courtship of the female. He gathers shells, small stones and other bits of "decoration" which he places nearby.

The crane, a large wading bird, builds its nest of grasses or weed stalks in a marsh or field.

The honey guide, a tropical forest dweller, feeds on bee larvae and honey, and with its noisy chatter it will guide men to a bee tree.

"perching tendon" in their legs. When these birds perch and their legs bend, this small tendon helps the toes to grasp the branch so they can sit or sleep without tiring themselves by holding tightly. The perching birds feed on seeds and insects. Belonging to this group are such well-known birds as sparrows, blackbirds, finches, jays and robins. Also in this group are the lyre bird, bird of paradise, humming-birds and parrots and their relatives.

Birds that eat flesh and hunt by day are known as birds of prey. They all have hooked beaks and powerful claws and find their prey—that is, the animals they eat—with their excellent eyesight. The largest birds of this type are the turkey vultures of America, which include the condors. The

the ground and lined with a few scraps of dried grass, like the plover's. More often it is a cup-shaped nest of grass or roots.

There are few birds that do not use a nest at all for their egg-laying. One is the

The brush-turkey of Australia builds a large mound of leaves as a nest. It lays its eggs inside the mound, where it is warm.

Andean condor of South America is the largest of all flying birds. Its wing-span of twelve feet is equal to that of the wandering albatross, which has a smaller body. They are called turkey vultures because, like turkeys, they have brightly-coloured fleshy decorations on their heads and bills.

Most birds build a nest of some sort, even if it is only a saucer shape scraped in

guillemot, a common sea-bird that lives along rocky coasts. The hen lays her one egg on the bare ledge of a cliff. The emperor penguin, which lives in Antarctica, also lays only one egg, and she and her mate take it in turns to hold the egg on their feet, so that it is not in contact with the ice.

Some birds use nests, but never build their own. The cuckoo is a well-known

The various positions of the wings of the ruby-throated hummingbird when they are in motion. In reality, the wings move so rapidly that they cannot be seen.

example of a bird that takes over the nest of another bird in this manner. Each hen cuckoo will lay her egg in the nest of a particular bird. One will visit only the nests of the meadow-pipit, laying one egg in each. Another one will choose the nests of hedge-sparrows. In each case, the cuckoo's egg will look very much like those of the bird that owns the nest. The cuckoo's egg usually hatches before the others and the young cuckoo then begins to shoulder the other eggs out of the nest. If the foster-mother's young hatch first, the young cuckoo, when it hatches, will push them to the rim of the nest and tip them out. The cuckoo is not trying to be cruel, all it is doing is making sure that it gets enough to eat.

The young cuckoo grows rapidly, and soon it is larger than its foster-parents, who are kept busy feeding it. While waiting to be fed it keeps up a continuous call, like the sound of someone pumping up a bicycle tyre. Any small birds passing overhead with food for their own young are likely to be attracted to the cuckoo and, strangely enough, will feed it! If they didn't, it is likely that many young cuckoos would starve.

The golden eagle, sometimes called the "King of Birds", is one of the swiftest and most majestic birds of prey. The eagle has been adopted as a national emblem in several countries.

The vulture, a native of both the Old World and the New, does not kill its prey but feeds on dead animals, or carrion.

The kestrel is a small falcon that feeds on beetles and other large insects, and field mice.

A peregrine falcon is a swift and expert bird of prey, and was prized during the Middle Ages as a trained hunting bird.

H. FERNANDEZ '60

By August the young cuckoo is ready to fly south, and nothing will stop it from trying to do so. It has never seen its real parents, but knows by instinct how to find its way to its winter quarters. The cuckoo is not the only bird to make yearly journeys, or migrations, to warmer climates, nor does it make the longest journey. Swallows travel further, but the longest journey is made by the Arctic tern, which spends the summer in the Arctic. When winter comes, the tern flies south to Antarctica. Since the seasons are reversed in the southern half of the earth, below the equator, it is summer in the Antarctic when the terns arrive. The journey is 11,000 miles each way, and yet these birds are able to find their way to the same spot each year. How do they find their way? By landmarks? Probably these help a great deal. Certainly, migrating birds follow definite routes, as though using landmarks, and they can lose their way in a fog. While we still cannot say for certain how they do it, we now know that they navigate using the sun by day and the stars at night. In recent years, studies have been made of the Adélie penguins of Antarctica, which travel hundreds of miles over the ice to spend the winter along the warmer edges of the Antarctic ice cap. Scientists believe that the penguins are guided by built-in "sun clocks" which tell them when to begin their journey and in which direction to go. Penguins, of course, do not fly, so they must make their way overland, swimming where there are patches of water, and walking and sliding over the ice. They do it in a spirit of great fun, and often march along in formation like little soldiers. Sometimes they slide along the ice on their bellies! After spending the winter in their temporary home, the penguins use their "sun clocks" once again to tell them when to start back, and they can time it so well that they usually arrive back in their breeding grounds just as summer begins.

As we have seen, the birds of the world are very different from one another in size, shape, colour and habit. The largest bird is the ostrich, which lives in the warm, sandy grasslands of southern Africa. It may be as much as 8 feet high, including its long neck, and may weigh up to 300 pounds. The hen ostrich usually lays about 15 eggs, each weighing about 3 pounds. One empty ostrich egg-shell is large enough to hold the contents of 15 eggs from an ordinary chicken! Other large birds are the cassowary of Australia and New Guinea, the emus of Australia, and the rheas of South America. Emus and rheas are ostrich-like birds and live in similar surroundings.

The smallest birds are the hummingbirds of America, some of which are no larger than a hawk moth. Their eggs are the size of large pearls. Flightless birds like the penguin are descended from flying birds that lost the power of flight but developed other abilities instead. Another unusual flightless bird is the kiwi, a wingless bird about the size of a chicken that lives in New Zealand. Since it cannot fly to escape from its enemies, it is able to run very quickly, and has sharp claws to protect itself if necessary.

The wandering albatross is one of the largest and most famous of flying birds. It can be up to 53 inches long and attain a wingspread of $11\frac{1}{2}$ feet. When flying through strong winds, albatrosses do not flap their wings but glide for hours at a time, settling on the water now and then to feed on cuttlefish and squid.

Cowboys and Indians

It may seem surprising, but the cowboys of today lead very much the same lives herding cattle in the American West as they did a hundred years ago. On some large ranches modern equipment like trucks and small aeroplanes are used to help track down and herd cattle, but most ranchers would agree that there is still no substitute for the cowboy on his well-trained horse.

In all his work the cowboy must rely a great deal on his horse, which, together with its rider, knows just how to keep a troublesome steer in order. A cowboy's main job, of course, is to make sure that the herd stays together, and he must round up any strays that wander off and drive them back to the main herd. Every spring the whole herd is rounded up and counted. The annual round-up is probably the busiest time of the year for the cowboy, for at that time any calves which have been born since the previous round-up must be counted and branded.

In order to brand the calves, the herd is driven into small enclosures, or corrals, and the calves are separated from their mothers for branding. This is not always

easy, for the calves often seem to know what is coming and make it difficult for the men to catch and hold them down. "Calf-throwing" is such a challenge, in fact, that it has become a featured event at many of the rodeos that are held each year.

The branding itself is done with a hot iron, which is made in a different shape for each ranch. When the iron is heated, it is pressed very quickly onto the calf's hide. Then the calf is released and allowed to rejoin its mother. The brand the calf carries will identify it in case it should be lost or stolen.

One of the things a cowboy looks forward to most each year is the rodeo, which is usually held in a town so that people from the surrounding area can attend. At the rodeo the cowboys show off their skill at roping, branding, riding wild steers, and bronco-busting. A "bronco" is a horse which has run wild ever since it was born. The taming, or breaking-in of broncos is usually done at the ranch, and takes quite

In the early days of the West, cowboys assisted in the long cattle drives from the open range to market. Covered wagons held provisions for the journey.

A Hopi dancer of the American South-west, dressed for his part in the rain-making ceremony. This is just one of the colourful dances which have been handed down since ancient times.

Pictured here are American Indians from just four of the many original tribes. Left to Right: *Sioux, Ojibva, Hopi and Blackfeet.* Each tribe has its own ceremonial costume.

a long time, but for the rodeo some of the broncos are specially rounded up for a contest in which men try to ride them. As the horses have never been ridden before, they twist and turn and rear and buck, and the cowboys that do stay on, even if only for a few minutes, are very good riders indeed.

When we think of cowboys, we often think of Indians as well, though in fact some cowboys today have never seen an Indian, and some Indians are cowboys themselves! There are, of course, many different Indian tribes living in various parts of America, not only in the West. Most of them live in the same way as other Americans—they work, go to school and serve in the armed forces along with everyone else. The largest group of Indians that have less contact with other Americans and still follow their own traditions are the tribes living in the south-western part of the country, in Arizona and New Mexico. These Indians are mainly from the Navajo, Hopi, and Zuni tribes; they live in small villages dotted about on large reservations—land which they have been given by the government. They raise sheep for a living, but since the flat, dry desert land is not well suited for grazing, it is difficult for the Indians to make a good living and many

of them are very poor. In recent years the government has been helping the Indians by building schools and health clinics and teaching them how best to use the little farmland they have.

The Indians are also being encouraged to preserve their traditions, especially their tribal dances and their arts and crafts. The pottery, woven rugs and silver jewellery made by the Indians are famous for their beauty and craftsmanship. The ancient art of sand painting has been handed down for generations, for the multi-coloured sands that make this desert landscape so lovely to look at also provide ready-coloured materials for painting. On a surface of flattened yellow sand, the Indian artist sifts his coloured sands into extraordinarily beautiful designs, most of which are full of religious symbols since the paintings were originally part of ancient rituals.

Well known to any tourist who has visited this part of America are the various tribal dances which the Indians perform, often as part of the entertainment at a rodeo or during special festivals during the summer. Vivid costumes, decorated with feathers and jewellery in bright colours, and the fearsome masks worn by the dancers make watching one of these rituals an unforgettable experience!

39

core

dense rock mantle

The Earth's Crust

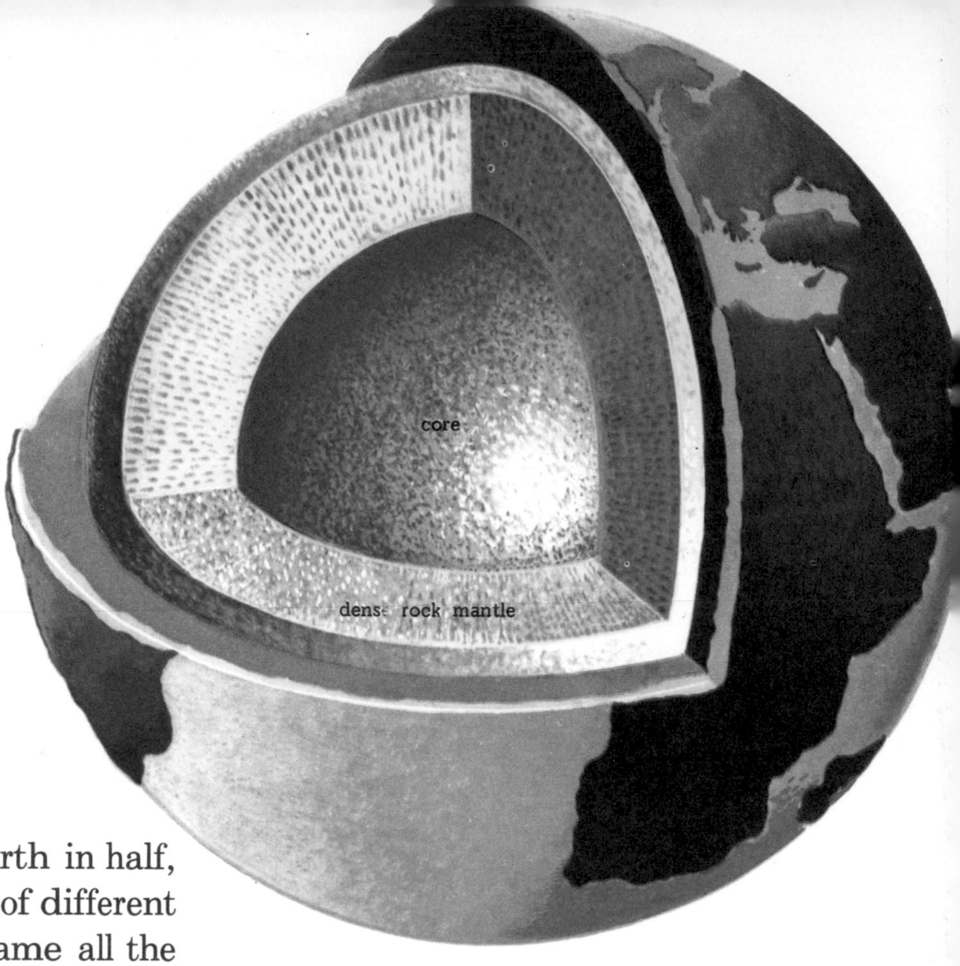

If it were possible to cut the earth in half, we would see that it is made up of different layers rather than being the same all the way to the middle. We cannot, of course, cut into the earth to see what's inside, so how *do* we know what it looks like?

Strangely enough, it is earthquakes that tell us. The shock waves sent out by earthquakes travel right through the earth and can be picked up by a delicate instrument, called a "seismograph", thousands of miles away. It is from an examination of what the seismograph records that scientists are able to tell the nature of the inside of the earth.

The most recent picture shows that the centre of the earth consists of a solid ball of metal, mostly iron, about 1,550 miles in diameter. This is called the "inner core". Outside this comes a layer of molten rock and metal 1,400 miles deep, and this is called the "outer core". Above this, the earth is solid again for 1,700 miles. This is called the "mantle" and it consists of heavy rock similar to the kind known on the surface as olivine. On top of the mantle come a few miles of basalt, with blocks of granite embedded in it, called the "crust".

It is the surface of the crust of the earth that forms all the different types of landscapes we know—mountains, valleys, canyons, plains, and hills. Each of these features has been formed over hundreds of thousands of years and the earth's surface is still changing, though so slowly that for the most part we cannot see it happen.

The earth's crust and its form is, to us, the most important part of our planet, for it is the natural features of the earth that decide how we will live and even what kind of weather we will have. The crust also contains all of our important minerals, as well as crude oil and natural gas.

If you have ever climbed a mountain, or even a high hill, you must have wondered how such a huge mass of rock or earth came to be raised to such a height. The original cause of all mountains must be sought a few miles down in the crust of the earth, where the rocks are squeezed together under enormous pressure. Those under the highest pressure gradually push the others out of the way, but they move very slowly—perhaps a fraction of an inch in a hundred years!

Some of them are pushed straight up,

Above: *A tornado* Left: *How rain is formed: as the clouds rise the vapour cools, condenses, and falls as rain.*

A typical rolling English landscape. Gentle hills such as these are often all that remain of a very old mountain range, worn down over the centuries.

Peaks and glaciers in the Andes. This mountain range stretches along the entire Pacific coast of South America, and its highest peak is Aconcagua, (28,080 feet), a volcano, now extinct, that lies on the border between Argentina and Chile.

*An aerial view of the forest and swamp in the Amazon basin,
the lowland area drained by the river and its tributaries.*

*An oasis near Marrakesh,
Morocco, showing the
canyon the water has
carved out of the desert.
In the background are
the Atlas Mountains.*

and raise the surface of the ground like a lift. Others are squeezed between huge blocks, and are buckled up or "folded" just as a carpet buckles up if you push it against a wall.

A range of hills is often merely an "old" mountain range which has become worn down over thousands of years to gentle, rolling land through the action of wind and water.

Caves and canyons are formed when water from underground or surface rivers wears away or dissolves the rock over which it flows. Streams flowing into the cracks and crannies of limestone rocks rapidly dissolve the rock and widen the cracks into caves. Quite often a river will dissolve such large holes in its bed that all its water is swallowed up and the river continues to flow underground. It may then dissolve out huge caves or chains of caves.

A canyon is formed in the first place by a river flowing across a desert, gradually cutting a V-shaped valley in the rock. Since there is no rain to wash the sides of the valley into the river, the valley grows deeper and deeper without becoming much wider, and a canyon is formed. The Grand Canyon, in the U.S.A., is over a mile deep, and its little river is still cutting its way down through the rock! Some of the weird shapes one sees in a canyon, (for example, the Bryce Canyon in the U.S.A.), are the results of weather—rain, frost, sunshine and wind. In the Bryce Canyon these have carved the rock into a forest of slender pillars of sandstone.

Every so often, pockets of molten rock in the crust of the earth are squeezed under pressure and find their way to the surface. A fountain of molten rock erupting from the earth is called a volcano. Volcanoes are found in those parts of the world where the earth's crust is thin and weak, or where the pressure happens to be exceptionally low under the wrinkles forming the great mountain chains. There are so many volcanoes round the coast of the Pacific Ocean that the region is sometimes called the "ring of fire".

The molten rock that comes out of a volcano is called "lava". Some of the lava shoots high into the air and falls as a terrible rain of red-hot stones and ashes, but other lava overflows and spreads over the land as a river of molten rock which moves slowly along like treacle. Wherever the lava falls or flows it destroys everything in its path, and sometimes whole towns are wiped out.

Although rivers are not strictly part of the earth's crust, they deserve mention because of the large part they play in changing and creating the shape of the face of the earth.

Rivers do three quite different kinds of work. They cut their channels downwards, they tend to spread out or wander about sideways, and they bring down vast quantities of sand and mud which they dump as soon as their speed slows down. They work very slowly but very surely, over tens and even hundreds of thousands of years.

We have already seen how a river can "build" a canyon out of stone. If a river passes over softer ground, however, it will make itself a wide valley, curving around hard rocks and wearing away the soft ones.

Japan is in the centre of the Far East earthquake belt. Of the 150 active volcanoes in the area, Fujiyama, on Honshu, is the most famous in Japan.

A roadway torn apart during an earthquake in Chile, caused by the sudden displacement of part of the earth's crust. Chile lies entirely within an earthquake belt—an area where the earth's crust is constantly shifting.

The Continent of Europe

A peasant family on their way to market in Transylvania, Romania. The horse and cart are still used in many parts of Europe.

Stretching from the Mediterranean Sea north to a point well inside the Arctic Circle is the continent of Europe. It includes many different countries, with many groups of people speaking a number of different languages. It has a variety of climates, from the frozen Arctic lands of northern Scandinavia to the sunny shores of the Mediterranean Sea.

If we start at the northern end of Europe, the first countries we come to are those in Scandinavia—Norway, Sweden, Denmark and Finland. Here the climate is generally cold, though along the coast of Norway the weather is warmer because of the warm ocean current, the North Atlantic Drift, that passes close to the land. Much of the jagged coastline of Norway was formed by great glaciers that moved down from the polar regions thousands of years ago. Where the deep valleys carved out by the glaciers reached the coast, they were filled by the sea, and the narrow, deep inlets that we know as *fjords* were formed.

The people of Scandinavia are descendants of the Norsemen, who were one of the first early peoples to explore the world around them. Sailing about in their sturdy ships, they raided the lands around the North Sea and were the first Europeans to see the New World. Today, though the Scandinavians stay closer to land, fishing is still a big industry, as is lumbering. Because of the climate and the mountainous landscape, farming is more difficult, and only in Denmark is it done on a large scale.

The country farthest east in Europe is Russia, which stretches across Asia so that it is really in two continents at the same time. Western Russia includes Moscow, the capital, and is the area where most of Russia's people live. They have come over the centuries from many parts of Europe and Asia, so that the people in Russia today are a mixture of many different races. When Russia was ruled by Czars, before 1918, most people in Russia tilled the soil for a living. Since the Russian Revolution in 1918, however, Russia has built up industries to process her natural resources, such as coal, oil, iron and manganese. Being such a large country, Russia contains many different landscapes and many different climates. The Ural Mountains run down the middle of the country, more or less dividing it in half. It is here that many mineral deposits are mined, while farming is mainly done on the flat prairie-

The colourful cathedral of St. Basil, which faces Lenin's tomb in Moscow. The building was begun by Ivan the Terrible in 1554 and is now used as a historical museum.

The vast forests of Scandinavia provide lumber and paper for people everywhere. These logs will be floated down the river to a lumber mill when the ice thaws.

The Sogne Fjord, on the west coast of Norway. These deep fjords cut into the mountains down the whole length of this northern land.

A view from the air of Trafalgar Square, London, with the church of St. Martin-in-the-Fields at centre left. In the background is the Thames, the river along which London is built.

like "steppes" of western Russia. We find yet another kind of Russian climate in the south, along the borders of Turkey and Iran, a semi-tropical region. The warm beaches along the Black Sea in this area have become very popular with holiday-goers.

To the north-west of mainland Europe lie the British Isles, which include England, Scotland, Wales, Northern Ireland and the Irish Republic. Because of the Gulf Stream, a warm ocean current that passes close to the land, the British Isles have a mild and wet climate that makes them very suitable for farming. England is rich in such minerals as coal and iron, the basic materials of her many industries. In the higher areas, such as Scotland and northern Wales, sheep and cattle raising take the place of crop growing. The fact that Britain is surrounded by water and carries on a busy trade with other countries means that she has a number of large and busy ports, among them Glasgow, Liverpool, and London, the capital of Great Britain.

Across the English Channel, on the mainland of the continent of Europe, is France. Paris, the capital of France and one of the most beautiful cities in the world, is a centre of culture and the arts which visitors from many parts of the world can enjoy. Many people also flock to the south of France for other kinds of enjoyment, for the Côte d'Azur along the Medi-

Northern Wales has some of the most magnificent mountain scenery in Europe, while the southern part of the country is much more heavily industrial, and is dotted with many factories and mines.

48

The Ile de la Cité in the middle of the River Seine, in Paris. Centre
right is the famous cathedral of Notre Dame. The embankment in the right
foreground is the Quai des Orfèvres leading to the Palais de Justice.

The Rhine near the Lorelei Rock, Germany. On the far bank are terraced vineyards.

A typical Dutch landscape in Polderland, where picturesque windmills keep the land drained of water.

Mont Blanc in the French Alps on the frontiers of France and Italy. The glacier in the foreground is Mer de Glâce, formed where the Giant Glacier (right) and the Leschaux Glacier (left), come together at bottom centre.

terranean boasts blue sky, clear warm water, and beautiful beaches.

Europe has many great rivers which for centuries have been important travel and trade routes. The valleys of some, such as the Rhône in France and the Ruhr in Germany have become great industrial centres. Others, like the Rhine River in Germany and the Danube, which flows through several countries, including Austria and Germany, have also inspired writers and composers with their beauty and colourful history. The Po River in northern Italy is surrounded by some of Italy's richest farmland, and is responsible for the growth of such cities as Venice, Milan, Padua and Mantua.

In the centre of Europe is the continent's largest mountain range, the Alps. These majestic peaks cover areas in Switzerland, France, northern Italy and Austria, and contain some of the highest mountains in Europe. Switzerland, a country that is almost entirely in the mountains, is probably the only European country that has been independent for centuries, since the Alps have always provided Switzerland with barriers against attacks from her neighbours. The Swiss can do very little farming but they use the high mountain pastures for grazing cattle and goats from which come Switzerland's famous cheeses. Because of the lack of space, the Swiss have had to concentrate on industries which use little space but special skills, such as watchmaking. The country is also a world banking and insurance centre, and is popular with tourists, who come from all over the world to climb the mountains or ski on their slopes. Famous peaks like the *Jungfrau* and the *Matterhorn* have for years attracted men who have attempted to conquer their heights.

In complete contrast to the mountains

Cattle grazing in the Swiss Alps. The herds are taken up to the higher pastures in the summer and are brought down into the valley each winter.

Cathedral of St. Peter's in Rome, the centre of the Roman Catholic Church. It is one of the many beautiful churches that were built during the Italian Renaissance.

of Central Europe are the lowlands to the north. If we look at a map of the Netherlands we can see that about one-fifth of the country lies below sea level. The combination of stormy weather and high tides in the North Sea could bring the waters high enough to flood half the country. The Dutch have been fighting the sea for centuries, and have devised wonderful schemes for dealing with their problem. As far back as the thirteenth century they were building enormous barriers, or dikes, to keep out the sea. They drained large areas of land, called "polders", and kept them from flooding again by building great windmills to pump out the water. Land continued to be reclaimed throughout the nineteenth century, but the greatest advances have come within the last fifty years. Two of the latest and most amazing drainage schemes are still to be completed—the Delta Project and the Zuyder Zee Works. When the Zuyder Zee project is finished, the farmland of the Netherlands will have been increased by about ten per cent, there will be new spaces for towns, new sites for industry, and new places for sailing,

The Greeks built temples to their gods all over the ancient world. This one, in Paestum, Italy, is in the style of the Parthenon in Athens.

swimming and sunbathing for the holiday-goers.

Along the coast of the Mediterranean Sea are the warm and sunny lands which were in ancient times the centres of Greek and Roman civilization. Today, relics of ancient Rome and art of mediaeval Italy and the Renaissance bring tourists from all over the world to Italy to see her treasures. Florence, probably the most beautiful of all Italian cities, contains so much for visitors to see that they often spend their entire holiday in the city, going to the many art galleries and looking at the magnificent buildings. A terrible tragedy occurred in 1966 when the waters of the Arno River, which flows through Florence, rose and flooded the city. Besides the human lives that were lost, many valuable and treasured works of art were swept away or destroyed beyond repair. People everywhere were so shocked at this that when the river went down again, experts and teams of volunteer workers from all over the world went to help the Florentines dig out their city from mud and tried to save works of art that were not too badly damaged. Many other people who could not come sent money to help pay for this work.

Greece today helps to supply the world with important crops such as olives and tobacco, which grow in her warm Mediterranean climate. More important, however, Greece has the many ancient buildings and monuments that have survived to tell us about the early Greeks, who contributed so much to our civilization. Much of Greece's wealth today comes from the thousands of tourists who go to visit these magnificent ruins. They go especially to Athens, Greece's capital, whose early citizens gave to the world the idea of democracy—the kind of society in which people govern themselves. The islands of Rhodes and Crete, off the coast of Greece, were at one time the sites of great cities, and they too have wonderful ruins for visitors to see. The Parthenon in Athens, which was in early times the Greeks' temple to the goddess Athena, is a beautiful example of classic Greek architecture.

At the western end of the Mediterranean Sea is the Iberian Peninsula, on which are Spain and Portugal. Though Spain is a European country, her landscape has far more in common with the North African countries that with the countries of central and northern Europe. Much of the land is dry and not very suitable for farming, and so a great part of Spain's wealth comes from the tourist industry. Beautiful scenery, ancient towns, and sunny beaches along the Mediterranean attract thousands of visitors each year.

Portugal, to the west of Spain, has enough green and fertile land so that over 40 per cent of its people are farmers. Fishing is also a large industry in Portugal, and in recent years more and more tourists have found Portugal an inexpensive and beautiful place for holidays. Tourists have also made the Balearic Islands popular. This group of islands in the Mediterranean include Majorca, Minorca and Ibiza; they are actually regarded as provinces by Spain. They have been inhabited by man since prehistoric times and were occupied by the Romans after the fall of Carthage.

Norsemen braved the heavy seas of the Atlantic in small
wooden sailing boats rowed by strong oarsmen. Always ready
for battle, both ship and men were armed against attack
and in preparation for their raids on coastal villages.

Exploring Our World

Ever since the first caveman crossed a mountain to see what lay on the other side, man has been curious about the world around him. Think how much of our planet would still be unexplored territory if men had been content to stay where they were!

Some of the earliest people to travel far over the oceans were the Phoenicians, the Egyptians, the Cretans, and the Carthaginians. Mostly they went in search of trade, but sometimes ships were sent out with the purpose of finding new trade routes and exploring unknown lands. The oldest traveller's report that has survived is that of the Carthaginian, Hanno. In 550 B.C. he led a huge fleet along the north and west coasts of Africa.

The first people to sail right across the Atlantic Ocean to the Americas were the Vikings, the sturdy, seafaring peoples of Scandinavia. There are few remaining records of these voyages, but we are fairly certain that the Norwegian, Eric the Red, founded the first European settlement in Greenland about 980 A.D. About twenty years later, Bjorne Herfuljson lost his way on a voyage to Greenland and sighted the American continent. Some time later another Norseman, Leif Ericson, landed on the eastern coast of America and "Vinland", as it was called, became the first European colony on American soil. It is thought that this colony was somewhere in the region of New Jersey or Virginia. The Vikings who settled there were continually attacked by the natives, and eventually they had to return home. Following this, the Vikings lost interest in the land they had discovered, and as time passed the existence of this new continent was completely forgotten.

Nearly 500 years passed before people began to be interested in venturing across the Atlantic again. During that time Europeans had discovered the riches in the Far East after Marco Polo made the journey overland to China in 1271. Christopher Columbus, a young navigator who was born in Genoa, Italy, about 1451, believed that a new way to India could be found by sailing in a westward direction. It took him years to convince others that this was possible, but he finally persuaded the King and Queen of Spain to help him. With three small ships Columbus made the long and dangerous voyage across the Atlantic and stepped ashore in the New World in October, 1492. He believed he had reached India, and called the islands he found the West Indies, and the people Indians.

In 1497 an Italian who had settled in England and who was known as John Cabot, sailed westwards with an expedition fitted out by Henry VII. Cabot was a

Ocean routes of some of the most famous navigators on their voyages of exploration. It was one thing to sail along the coast in small wooden ships, but to set out across the uncharted ocean with its heavy seas and treacherous currents required great skill and daring.

Vikings

Pytheas

Cook's first voyage

Vasco da Gama

Magellan

Hanno

superb navigator, and sailing on a more northerly course than Columbus, he reached North America after a voyage of about eight weeks. Like Columbus, Cabot believed he had landed in Asia. It was another Italian, Amerigo Vespucci, who realized that the so-called India was, in fact, a different continent. To this day it bears his Christian name, though Columbus or Cabot perhaps deserve the honour far more!

Once these brave explorers had led the way, many others followed. Sebastian Cabot, the son of John, sailed through the Hudson Strait and explored Hudson Bay. Vincente Yanez Pinzon, who had been captain of one of Columbus's ships, and Juan Diaz de Solis both crossed the equator. The Portuguese, Pedro Alvarez Cabral, was accidentally blown westwards to America and landed in Brazil. He claimed the territory for Portugal, and even today the language spoken in Brazil is Portuguese.

People in search of riches, adventure or a new life flocked westwards in greater numbers. In 1513 Vasco Nuñez de Balboa of Spain made a land crossing of the Isthmus of Panama, and was the first explorer to set eyes on the Pacific Ocean. Hernando Cortez of Spain conquered the Aztec people of Mexico; Francisco Pizarro with his small army marched through Peru and established himself as ruler of the Inca empire.

Long before Australia had been discovered by Europeans, geographers were including a huge land area on their maps

which they labelled *Terra Australis*. Part of the area was indeed Australia, and the story of the discovery of this part of the world therefore lies in the gradual trimming down of this large, imaginary continent.

The Dutch were the first to make the Australian continent known to the West. In 1605 the Dutch East India Company sent Captain William Janszoon out to chart the island of New Guinea, and he sailed into the Gulf of Carpentaria on the northern coast of Australia.

Ten years after this a Dutchman named Dirk Hartog reached the west coast of Australia, and in 1642 Van Diemen, the Governor General of the Dutch East Indies, sent Captain Abel Janszoon Tasman to find out more about this great new land that was beginning to be known as "New Holland". Tasman voyaged so far southeast that he missed Australia and eventually reached the west coast of Tasmania. After this he sailed eastwards until he arrived at the South Island of New Zealand.

The man who did most toward the mapping of both Australia and New Zealand was an Englishman, Captain James Cook. Sailing round New Zealand, Cook made charts of the two islands and the waters surrounding them, and then sailed to Australia. Reaching the eastern coast where no other European had been before, he claimed part of it for England and named it "New South Wales". In 1772 Cook was put in

When Tasman's ships anchored off the coast of New Zealand, the Maori natives excitedly gathered together to look at this strange new arrival—the white man.

charge of another expedition. This mission took three years, during which time Cook was able once and for all to establish the true positions of both Australia and New Zealand.

One of the most remarkable voyages in exploration of the waters of the earth was an expedition along nearly the entire length of the Amazon River in South America, headed by Francisco de Orellana. In the early part of the 16th century, Orellana was accompanying a party under Gonzalo Pizarro who was looking for a land rich in gold that was said to be east of Ecuador. Crossing the Andes Mountains, hundreds of men died of the cold and exhaustion, and when they finally reached the Napo River, Pizarro ordered Orellana to go ahead by boat and search for food. Little did Orellana realize that he was setting out on one of the most amazing journeys of all time. The Napo eventually joined up with another, much larger river. Intense heat, snakes and swarms of fierce insects were just a few

Dense masses of trees, tall ferns and twining vines were all Orellana and his party could see on the long journey down the Amazon River.

One of the Portuguese explorers' ships sailing down the coast of Africa in the 15th century meets a small party of West Africans paddling along in a dug-out canoe.

of the hardships Orellana and his men suffered, and there was continual threat of attack from the natives who lived in the damp, steamy jungle along the banks. Eventually, they reached the Atlantic Ocean, after having sailed 3,000 miles in something like seven months!

One of the men who did most to further exploration of the world's oceans was a prince of Portugal who became known as "Henry the Navigator". He fitted out expeditions across the Atlantic and down

the west coast of Africa. The knowledge gained by two of Henry's explorers, Diaz and Covilha, was of great use to the next great Portuguese explorer, Vasco da Gama. In 1497 da Gama was sent out to search for an eastern route to India. He sailed around the Cape of Good Hope at the southern tip of Africa and reached India in May of 1498. Probably the greatest Portuguese explorer and navigator of all was Magellan. Enlisting the help of the King of Spain, Magellan set out in 1519 to sail round the world. Crossing the Atlantic, Magellan sailed south and through the narrow, winding straits at the tip of South America that now bear his name. Unfortunately, Magellan himself was killed crossing the Pacific by natives of the Philippine Islands, but under Sebastian del Cano one ship in the expedition completed the voyage as originally planned. His ship reached Seville in Spain on September 8, 1522.

The continent of Africa was one of the last regions of the world to be explored, though its coastal areas had been known since the time of the ancient Egyptians and Phoenicians. Arab traders had ventured inland in search of gold and slaves, but very little otherwise was known of this vast area until the 18th and 19th centuries.

Two of the earliest of the African explorers were James Bruce and Mungo Park, but the two who are remembered

Livingstone discovered the Victoria Falls on the 17th of November 1855. His first view of the magnificent waterfall was from the island that now bears his name.

*Victoria Falls, in Central Africa, is one
of the most spectacular sights in the world.
Every minute, from 62 to 100 million gallons
of water pour over its edge into the chasm.*

above all others are Dr. David Livingstone and Henry Morton Stanley. Dr. Livingstone travelled a great deal in Africa as explorer and missionary. He crossed the Great Kalahari Desert to Lake Ngami, discovered the Upper Zambezi River and Victoria Falls, and explored Lakes Nyasa, Tanganyika and the river Luapula. In 1866 Livingstone set out to try and find the source of the Nile River. For months nothing was heard from him, and finally the *New York Herald*, an American newspaper, sent Henry Morton Stanley, a young reporter, to look for him. Stanley actually did succeed in finding Livingstone, who was in very poor health, and stayed with him for four months. When Stanley finally left, Livingstone remained behind to live out the last eighteen months of his life in the land to which he had given so much of his time.

After Livingstone's death Stanley carried on with the work of exploration. His most important expedition was made in 1874, when he sailed round the shores of Lake Victoria and navigated the course of the river Lualaba. On the way down the river, the boats often had to be dragged or carried through the dense forest on either side of the river to avoid dangerous rapids and whirlpools. The party of men was reduced to a fraction of its original number through hardships which included battles with the natives, many of whom were cannibals. The party struggled on, however, and eventually came to another river which flowed into the mighty Congo. At last Stanley learned that the sea was only five days away. On August 12, 1877, two and a half years after setting out from the east coast of Africa, the survivors of the expedition reached Boma, on the western coast. They had travelled right across the continent!

The first exploration of the Arctic regions took place when, in the 16th century, explorers began searching for a northern passage to China. It was not until 1773 that an expedition of two ships under the command of C. T. Phipps set out with the purpose of discovering the position of the North Pole, but this expedition was a failure, as were many others that followed. In 1893 a Norwegian doctor, Fridjof Nansen, sailed to the Arctic. When his ship froze in the ice, Nansen trekked across the sea ice with dog sledges, but was forced to turn back two hundred miles from the Pole. In 1909, Robert Peary, a young American naval officer, set out for the North Pole. When the expedition was only 130 miles away from the Pole, Peary left the main party and with four Eskimos and his Negro servant, he reached the North Pole on April 6, 1909.

The first real expedition to the Antarctic was made by Captain James Clark Ross in about 1840. Sixty years later the next major attempt was made when Shackleton got within 120 miles of the South Pole. The honour of reaching the Pole itself goes to Roald Amundsen, who arrived on December 14, 1911, just one month before Robert Scott.

Exploration in the polar regions is still going on, for there is much we still do not know about these icy lands. In 1958, the atomic-powered submarine U.S.S. *Nautilus* made a voyage under the Arctic ice cap to try and find new and faster sea routes for cargo ships. In the same year a number of stations for scientific study were set up in the Antarctic. As part of the investigation of such things as weather, sea life, plant life, mineral deposits and ocean currents, Dr. Vivian Fuchs led an exploring expedition across the frozen continent from Shackleton Base to Scott Base on the Ross Sea.

The Danish arctic ship Magga Dan *smashes her way through the ice of the Weddell Sea.*

The World of Fishes

All fishes belong to the class of animals we call *vertebrates*—that is, animals with backbones. Fishes are different from all other vertebrates in that they live their entire lives under water and have gills instead of lungs for breathing. Most fishes have a torpedo-shaped body, covered with scales, which is propelled by a tail and balanced by fins.

The body of a fish consists of a head, trunk and tail. Where the head meets the trunk are the gills. The trunk is joined to the tail with little to show where one ends and the other begins. The head of a fish carries the sense organs. The snout, which is the part lying in front of the eyes, has a pair of nostrils on either side, for fishes have a very strong sense of smell. The eyes are placed on the sides of the head, and are specially constructed for seeing under water. It is not easy to see where a fish's ears are from the outside, but the inner ear,

inside the head, is a true organ of hearing. The inner ear also contains organs which help the fish to keep its balance, but the ear is also used for detecting sounds in the water. Many fishes actually do make noises of their own, although they do not have voices.

One reason fishes do not have ears on the outside of their heads is that ears would interfere with their streamlined shape. It is much easier for an object to move through the water if it is smooth, narrow and long, and everything in a fish's body is shaped to this end. Because fish are so streamlined and move so well through water, men have copied their shape in building submarines, torpedoes, and the like. A fish's eyes are flat on the surface of its head, and its snout is pointed, to make a cutwater. The fins can be folded in to lie flat against the body, and although the fish is covered with scales, they too lie flat.

ong believed to be extinct,
the coelacanth, a "living
ossil", has recently been
und in the Indian Ocean. It
believed that it was from
ese ancient fish that the
rst amphibians evolved.

*A lion, or scorpion, fish grows
to about a foot in length,
and the spines with which it
is covered are said to be
poisonous to its enemies.*

*The spitting fish is able to shoot a thin
jet of water at its insect prey, thereby
knocking the insect into the water, where
the fish can quickly gobble it up.*

A fish swims by waggling its tail. At the hind end of its body is a tail fin. The tail itself is that part of the body lying between the rear of the trunk and the tail fin. When a fish wants to swim quickly, it moves its tail rapidly from side to side, driving the body forward. The fins lying along the middle line of the back and under the tail act like the keel of a boat to keep the fish upright and on an even course. These fins are sometimes used for gentle movement forward. On the underside of the trunk there are also two pairs of fins which have slightly different uses. The pelvic fins, located toward the hind end of the fish, help to keep balance. The pectoral fins, further forward, are sometimes used for actual swimming, but in most fishes they serve for balancing, braking and steering.

To breathe, a fish takes water into its mouth which passes through the gills and is squirted out of the gill slits just behind the head. The gills contain a network of

67

very fine blood vessels lying just under the very thin skin. As the water passes over the gills, oxygen is taken out of the water and into the blood. At the same time carbon dioxide, a waste product, is passed into the water and carried away when the water leaves the fish's body. The surfaces of the gills are folded or feathery so that there is a larger area exposed to the water and more oxygen can be taken in. The squirting action that takes place when the water passes out through the gill slits also helps in moving the body of the fish forward. It is, in fact, a simple type of jet propulsion such as that used in jet-driven boats and planes.

A fish has another organ connected with swimming which is inside its body. A long bag of silvery membrane called a swim bladder lies along the fish's gut. It can be filled with or emptied of air, and is used by the fish for swimming at different depths. When the bladder is full, it acts rather like a child's rubber ring and pushes the fish up toward the surface of the water. If the fish wants to go down again, it lets some of the air out of the bladder, and is thus able to swim deeper more easily.

Some fishes feed on other fishes or on smaller animals such as worms, whelks, prawns, and the like. Other fishes feed on the minute, usually microscopic plants and animals near the surface of the water. These creatures are called plankton, and the fishes feeding on them are called plankton-feeders. Other fishes feed on vegetation. The size and shape of the teeth of a fish depend on what it eats. Plankton-feeders therefore have the smallest teeth, and fish that eat other fish have the largest. Good examples of those with large teeth are the pike, which has long, pointed teeth and a wide, gaping mouth, and the sharks. The piranha, or riverwolf, of South America, has teeth as sharp as razors. Although a piranha is not a large fish, a group of them together can strip the flesh of a dead pig lying in the water in no time.

The scales of fishes are arranged in overlapping layers, like tiles on a roof. In some, such as eels, the scales are so small and so deep in the skin that the fish seems to be without them. In others, like the sturgeon, the scales are larger and give the fish the appearance of being clothed in armour. It is possible to tell the age of some fishes by looking at the rings of the scales, just as it is possible to tell the age of a tree by looking at the rings in the wood. In winter, when food is scarce, the growth of the scale is slow and the rings are spaced far apart. In the summer, however, the scale grows more quickly and the rings are much closer together. The scale gradually becomes marked with areas that are lighter where the rings are farther apart and darker where they are close together. One can then count the number of winters and summers the fish has lived through.

An ordinary fish, like the herring, lives in groups, or shoals, of immense numbers. At a certain time of year, called spawning time, the females lay their eggs in the water and the males shed their milt over the eggs to fertilize them. The eggs sink to the bottom to lie on the sand and the parents take no further notice of them. The eggs of the sprat, which is like the herring in its

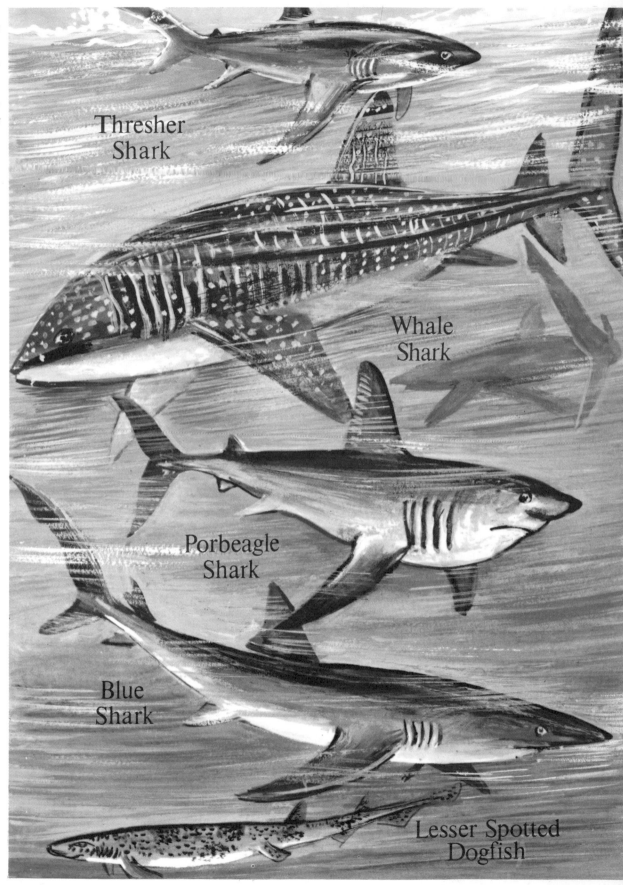

The sharks are the biggest members of the fish family. The largest of all is the whale shark, which may grow to a length of fifty feet or more.

Thresher Shark

Whale Shark

Porbeagle Shark

Blue Shark

Lesser Spotted Dogfish

habits, float near the surface of the water instead of sinking. Fish like these, that leave their eggs unprotected, must lay many more eggs at a time, for a great number of them will be eaten before they even have a chance to hatch. Each female herring lays about 50,000 eggs a year; the cod lays 6,000,000, the turbot 9,000,000 and the ling 15,000,000 eggs each year. Not all parent fish are as careless about looking after their offspring, however. In many species one or both parents spend a fair time each season guarding and caring for their eggs and for the young that hatch from them. Some fish build nests—the common stickleback is one; it uses lengths of grass or other water plants as building material. Some fish, like the butterfish, lay their eggs in rounded masses and one of the parents, usually the male, coils its body around the eggs to protect them.

Fishes come in many different colours, and usually their colouring serves some purpose, such as that of protection. The more familiar fishes are generally dull in colour, such as the herring. With this colouring they are better able to protect themselves since they match the rocks and

undersea plants around which they hide. In all fishes, however, the colours usually become brighter during the breeding season. Some fish put on special breeding colours—the red throat of the common stickleback is an example. This, like the red breast of a robin, is used in courting the female as well as in threatening enemies. As a rule, however, bright colours are much more common among tropical fishes, which live in colourful surroundings.

Coral-reef fishes are very brightly coloured, so that as long as they remain still they are very difficult to see against the bright masses of coral. This ability of fishes and other animals to look like their surroundings is called "camouflage", from the French word for "disguise".

Camouflage is sometimes assisted by the shape of a creature's body. There is a seahorse living in Australian waters that is not only coloured to match the seaweed around it, but also has loose flaps of skin on its body which float around the fish and make it look like a piece of seaweed itself! The fishes living in the Sargasso Sea, a large mass of weed in the western Atlantic, are remarkably like the seaweeds in form and colour.

Perhaps we may finish this entry on fishes with a few interesting figures. The largest fish known is the whale shark of the tropics, which grows to a length of fifty feet or more and weighs several tons. The basking shark of the colder seas may be up to forty feet long. Strange as it may

Rays, like the spotted eagle ray shown here, move through the water with graceful, wing-like flying movements.

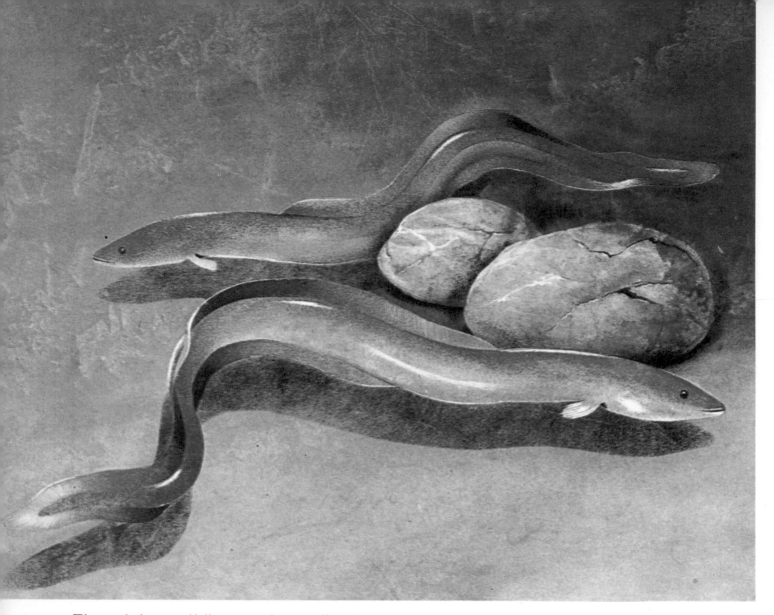

The eel does a "disappearing act" when it goes to the Sargasso Sea to spawn. Only the young eels, or elvers, return to populate the rivers of Europe.

seem, these giants are plankton-eaters, and though they have many teeth, each tooth is little bigger than the head of a pin. The largest of the meat-eating sharks, those with sharp, triangular teeth, are the blue sharks, which are nearly as large as the basking sharks. The smallest of all fishes is the goby, which lives in the lakes on the island of Luzon, in the Philippines. It is only half an inch long.

How long do fishes live? This is a very difficult question to answer. The white goby lives only one year, and at the other extreme, there are stories of carp that have lived for 150 years. These may be exaggerations, but it is possible that carp may live 50 or 60 years.

Speed? Well, the fastest swimmers are the sail-, spear-, and swordfishes, which have been timed at speeds of over 60 m.p.h. This is interesting when compared with the top speeds of several other fishes: the blue shark, 27 m.p.h.; the salmon, 25 m.p.h.; and the stickleback, 7 m.p.h.

Until fairly recently, zoologists believed that the depths of the seas were almost empty of life. The Barton bathysphere pioneered the way in underwater research. In the glare from its powerful light some of the strange creatures that inhabit the ocean's depths can be seen. It descended to a depth of a quarter of a mile.

The Common Tree Frog is able to change its colour to match its surroundings.

Frogs and Toads

To many people, frogs and toads look very much alike, but in fact they are very different animals. They are both amphibains—animals that can live on land and in the water—but toads spend most of their lives on land while frogs prefer the water.

There are other ways of recognizing the differences between frogs and toads. Most toads have a rough, moist skin, while frogs have a smooth, damp skin. Some toads have poison glands in their skin which help to protect them from attacks by other animals. One very large toad, called the Colorado River toad, has such a powerful poison that dogs attacking it have been known to die from the effects.

Frogs and toads can live almost anywhere where there is a warm summer and enough fresh water for their needs. While frogs live in and around ponds and streams, toads like fields and woods and only need water when it comes time to lay their eggs. Both frogs and toads lay eggs, called spawn, which are enclosed in jelly and float near the surface of the water. The little creatures that hatch from these eggs do not look at all like their parents: they are, at first, like little black blobs with long tails. They are called tadpoles, and spend the first part of their lives in the water, feeding greedily on water plants. As they grow bigger, little hind legs and then forelegs appear, and gradually their tails grow shorter. When they climb out of the water, they look just like their parents, only smaller.

Many frogs and toads have rather strange habits. One type, called a midwife toad, carries its eggs on its back. Some tropical frogs even carry their tadpoles on their backs! The male carries them, arranged in neat little rows, to a pond or stream where they can find their own food.

74

The male Midwife Toad takes charge of the eggs, carrying them on his back until they hatch.

The female South American Tree Frog carries her eggs on her back until they hatch as fully-developed frogs.

Tree frogs all have feet with broadened toes that are well-adapted to their climbing existence.

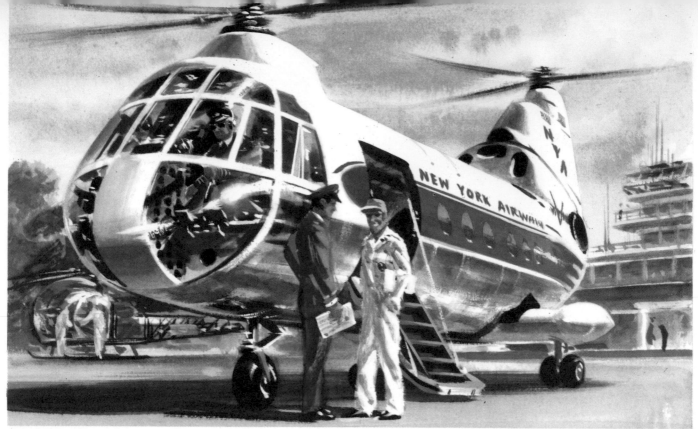

Helicopters

The first real helicopter flight was made by the Frenchman, Louis Breguet, in 1907. However, the honour of designing and building the first really successful helicopter goes to Igor Sikorsky, a Russian-American aircraft engineer who developed one of the leading aircraft industries in the United States. In 1940 one of the first helicopters made its trial flight, having been designed and built by Sikorsky.

This most unusual form of aircraft depends entirely on its rotary blades to lift it and move it forward. These blades are attached to a vertical shaft and rotate like an enormous flat propeller on the top of the craft. One of the earlier steps in the development of the helicopter as we know it today was the "autogyro". This flying machine had rotary blades, but they were only for lifting the craft off the ground. To move it forward or back, there was an engine at the front which powered an ordinary propeller. In a helicopter, on the other hand, both the lift and the forward movement are provided by the power-driven rotary blades. These blades can be tipped so that the circle they make when whirling can be set at different angles. In this way the movement of the helicopter is controlled, and it can move up, down, from side to side, forward or back, and can even hover in place.

Because the helicopter can take off from a standing position by going straight up in the air it has a great advantage over ordinary aircraft since it doesn't need a runway for take-off or landing. It can squeeze into spaces that would be too small for other aeroplanes, for all it requires to land is enough room around it so that its blades can rotate freely.

This wonderful feature of helicopters

Military helicopters have performed daring feats during wartime carrying troops and equipment to remote battle areas and removing the wounded.

makes them extremely useful for all sorts of tasks. Wherever there is no airfield and quick action is needed, helicopters are called in. There is no doubt that their most important jobs have been in air-sea rescue work. One interesting kind of air-sea "rescue" helicopters perform is in the area of space exploration. Yes, even here they have a job! When a manned spacecraft returns from its orbit and drops down into the ocean, a helicopter is ready to pick up the astronauts from their rubber rafts and carry them to a ship waiting nearby. Other types of emergency work a helicopter can do include rescuing mountaineers, lowering medical and food supplies to people stranded by floods or earthquakes, and fighting forest fires.

Helicopters also have many military uses. They can carry troops and equipment right into a battle zone and drop them wherever they are needed. A military version of the American "Vertol 107" can carry 40 troops. The "Belvedere" will carry 25 troops and 12 wounded on stretchers. The "Whirlwind" flies with the Royal Navy on anti-submarine work and with the Army Air Corps and the Royal Marines. It is also the R.A.F.'s rescue helicopter.

One of the newest uses to which these "whirlybirds" have been put is providing shuttle services between large airports and the cities they serve. Kennedy International Airport, which serves New York City, has such a service which runs from the airport to a special landing platform on the top of one of the tall skyscrapers in the centre of the city. Whereas it would take nearly an hour to get to the same place by ordinary means of transportation from the airport, the trip by helicopter takes 15 minutes!

Horses and Ponies

When we think of the size of a horse it is difficult to believe that the first horses were quite small creatures, measuring just under a foot or so high. In the thousands of years since that time, horses have grown and developed into the magnificent animals we know today.

Horses can be divided into many groups, according to their size and the type of work they do. Of course each group includes horses of many different breeds. The very large horses that are used for heavy work are usually called "draught" or "cart" horses, and the most important types include horses of Dutch, German, French, English and Austrian breeds. The ancestors

The chargers of the Middle Ages had to be strong enough to carry a knight in full armour.

Horses in a mounted cavalry regiment of an army in the nineteenth century.

Above left: *A soldier's well-trained mount of the eighteenth century.* Right: *the spirited horse belonging to a cavalier of the seventeenth century.*

of many of these horses were the chargers of the Middle Ages. For instance, the Shire, which is a very large horse, has as its ancestor the old English Great Horse, which was used for carrying knights, wearing full armour, into battle. The Percheron, on the other hand, was once used for drawing stage coaches. It is native to La Perche, in France, from where it gets its name.

Much smaller in size than the cart horse, but still strongly built, are the harness horses. A horse that will go into harness must have a good trotting action, for this is the pace most used when the horse is drawing a vehicle.

Finally, there is the saddle horse, which is much lighter and more streamlined than the harness horse. Some of the best known types of saddle horse are the Arab, the English Hunter and the American Gaited Saddle Horse.

Although motor-cars, trains and aircraft have now taken over much of the horse's work, the horse once provided the most important form of transport in the world. Not only did it carry people from place to

The Romans were among those who used the horse to help them in their many conquests.

A nineteenth century gentleman on his sleek English Hunter with its tail fashionably cropped.

place, but at various times it has drawn chariots, coaches, carts, fire-engines and even buses. Without horses, the conquests of vast empires would never have been possible, for soldiers could not have travelled as far on foot as they did on horseback. The early settlers who went to America would have found it very difficult to travel with all their belongings if they had not had horses to pull their wagons. The American Indian warrior and troops of cavalry relied on their horses completely, both for everyday use and in time of battle. Today, though machines have generally taken over the horses' work, there are still many things that a horse can do better than mechanical invention. Horses are used on the plains of North and South America, Australia and New Zealand for rounding up herds of cattle and sheep and for the inspecting of

The jumping is one of the main events in a gymkhana. There are usually about half a dozen different jumps included in the course.

herds and fences on large ranches. Horses are still used by the police in many countries, and they may still be seen, though in fewer numbers, pulling milk or coal carts.

A pony is a breed of small horse. Every type of pony looks different, but once you know what the differences are for each breed you can tell, almost at a glance, which breed it belongs to. Often breeds of ponies are named after the district they come from. The Dales pony lives in the Dales region of northern England. These sturdy little ponies are heavily built, and are famous for their strength and surefootedness. They have a quantity of fine hair on their heels. Bred for carrying loads, these ponies are not usually ridden. Years ago they were used a great deal for carrying the metal ores from the mines of Northumberland and Durham to the villages around, but now they are used mainly for harness

Many ponies live together in a semi-wild state until they are rounded up to be sold and trained.

work. The Fell pony comes from the fells of Westmorland and Cumberland and is similar to the Dales pony. Although these ponies, like the Dales, were first bred for carrying heavy loads, they are now very popular as children's riding ponies. They can be dark brown, dark bay and black, and sometimes dun on grey. Fell ponies are strongly built and have a rather shaggy coat with long hair around the jaw. Highland ponies are useful as riding, driving and pack ponies. There are two types of Highland pony, one of which is much larger and heavier than the other. The lighter type is usually found in the Hebrides, where it works as a pack pony, while the larger type is used mainly for farm work.

The Shetland pony is very well known and easy to recognize, for it is the smallest breed of pony in the world. It belongs to the same group as those that are found in Iceland and Northern Norway and its islands. This pony's small size does not make it any less strong than a bigger pony. It is tough and will live a long time, besides being intelligent and easy to manage.

Welsh ponies have lived wild or semi-wild in the Welsh mountains since pre-historic times, and are very good as children's ponies. The New Forest pony is also one of the best ponies for children to ride. New Forest ponies run loose while they are young in the New Forest in the South of England, and so they become quite used to cars and people. This makes them very steady for riding through traffic or crowds later on. Most of these ponies are bay or brown in colour.

Most ponies live in cool or temperate regions of the world, although there are exceptions to this, such as the Batak or Deli ponies which are found in Sumatra. Related to the Shetland pony are the Iceland and Norwegian ponies. The Iceland pony is not a native of the country; it was probably brought in at one time from Norway. It is gentle and affectionate, extremely tough and is usually grey or dun in colour. The Norwegian pony is hard-working and tireless, and is mostly used for pulling small carts.

A steeplechase, or a race with jumps, is a very popular type of sport. The best-known steeplechase is probably the Grand National, which is run regularly each year in Great Britain.

Pony trekking has become more and more popular with holiday-goers, who enjoy roaming the countryside on horseback. Pony treks can last from one day to two weeks or more; they are great fun for anyone who loves ponies and an open-air life.

The Hovercraft

Think how much faster and smoother a drive would be if the wheels of a car didn't have to touch the ground, and you will have some idea of the usefulness of one of the newest means of travel—the hovercraft.

The first hovercraft had its trial run in the Solent, the straits between England and the Isle of Wight, in 1959. It looked rather like a very broad, flat-bottomed boat with a wide funnel in the centre. Every hovercraft has a funnel of some sort, but these funnels are not smoke-stacks. Instead, they contain fans that draw in air and force it down through the craft and out of holes in the bottom. The air fills in the space underneath the craft in such a way that it cannot escape to the sides, and as more and more air is forced into this space, pressure builds until it is strong enough to lift the whole craft about 15 inches off the ground, where it hovers safely on its cushion of air. It can now be driven along by means of propellers or jets on the sides of the vessel, which are run on some of the high-pressure air from the fan.

Because it is raised off the ground, the hovercraft moves equally well over rough or smooth surfaces, and especially over water. The cushion of air raises it above anything that might get in the way; it rides over hills, bumps and waves, always keeping a constant height above the surfaces, whatever their shape. It can travel over a rough field, onto a beach and continue out to sea with no trouble at all. Hovercraft are, in fact, very similar to "amphibious" animals like frogs and turtles, that can live equally well on land or in the water.

The first hovercraft was 30 feet long and 24 feet across and travelled at about 30 miles per hour, but much greater speeds are possible. For a vehicle its size, the hovercraft can move more easily than a car

A military hovercraft on patrol. This type of craft can operate in areas where no other type of vessel can; for example, swamps, unnavigable rivers and deserts.

A passenger-carrying hovercraft of the type used for trips of about 30 to 50 miles.

on land, and on the sea it can out-do many ships. A hovercraft need not worry about tides, shallows, or rocks under the water, and it needs no special harbour.

Although the development of the hovercraft is still in its early stages, the craft has already been put to use. British Railways have been establishing a passenger hovercraft service between England and France during the summer months. The journey across the Channel by hovercraft is much shorter and smoother than it is on a Channel steamer. Smaller ferries have been designed, and include a 25-

tonner for use between the mainland and the Isle of Wight or the Isle of Man. This vessel can carry 68 passengers and 10 tons of freight at 80 miles per hour. A still smaller craft called the "cushion-craft" has been designed especially for crossing rough country that would be too bumpy for ordinary vehicles.

Looking even further ahead, engineers are hoping that one day hovercraft as large as ocean liners will be able to cross the Atlantic at 150 miles per hour. The journey to New York would take only 24 hours and would be much more comfortable than a liner or an aeroplane. Hovercraft should be ideal for services across such vast uninhabited regions as the centre of Australia. Aeroplanes cannot carry heavy cargoes and can only land where there are airports. The hovercraft can carry heavy loads almost anywhere and can stop on any patch of land or water. In fact, a modern exploring expedition made use of the hovercraft in 1967 when it was used to carry an expedition up the Orinoco River in Venezuela.

India and the Far East

India and the Far East are on the continent of Asia, the largest continent in the world. Asia is bounded on the east by the Pacific Ocean, on the south by the Indian Ocean, and on the north by the Arctic Sea. To the west are Russia and the Near East, though a great part of Russia runs into northern Asia. The continent is so vast that it contains every kind of climate, from the cold arctic lands of northern Siberia to the steaming jungles of Malaya in South-east Asia.

India is the seventh largest country in the world, and juts out into the Indian Ocean from the southern part of the Asian continent. Even in India climates vary, for the Himalayan Mountain range, that includes the highest peaks in the world, runs through northern India, while the people in the lower southern regions live in a hot, tropical climate. The Ganges River, one of the largest rivers in Asia, flows down from the mountains through India to the sea. It is considered by many Indians to be a holy river, and thousands of people make pilgrimages to Benares to bathe in its waters.

India is the home of a mixture of many

An open market in Southern India. The produce is laid out in great baskets or on the open ground. Each family sells the goods they have brought.

86

The crowded city of Benares on the Ganges River. Thousands of people make pilgrimages to Benares to pray and to bathe in the river. They consider its water to be holy and believe it has healing powers.

Water buffaloes such as these in the Indus River, have been tamed into gentle creatures. They are kept by the Indians for the milk they give and for pulling heavy things such as ploughs and carts.

different races of people, most of whom belong to one of the two main religions, Hinduism and Buddhism. Hinduism includes the worship of many gods, but more important, it divides people up into superior and inferior groups, or "castes", which has meant that all people are not treated equally. However, the caste system has now been outlawed by the government, and the Indian Constitution states that no one may give preference to a person just because he is of a higher caste.

Although India and her neighbour, Pakistan, are mainly agricultural countries, where people live by farming, some industry does exist. India is also rich in minerals and has recently been found to have some oil reserves as well. While India has a strong voice in the world of nations and is even taking part in the exploration of space, she has one major problem—too many people. India's population is far larger than her supply of food, and therefore millions of Indians do not eat properly. The government has launched a far-reaching programme to help keep India's population from growing too quickly, and to help her produce more food; this programme has so far been very successful.

India contains a great deal of beautiful and varied scenery, and there are many magnificent ancient buildings that a visitor may see. One of the most famous of these is the Taj Mahal, built by Shah Jehan about 1630 as a tomb and monument for his wife. It is said that it took 20,000 men 22 years to build the tomb and decorate it with the delicate carvings that cover the building.

Many animals live in India that are not

Chinese peasants plow a rice paddy on a commune in Yunnan, South China. Like the Indians, the Chinese use water buffaloes to pull their ploughs.

Villages in Nepal are laid out on the southern slopes of the Himalayas. The highest peak in the mountain range at the rear is Annapurna.

The Yangtze River, one of the main transportation routes in China, is full of busy river traffic including large junks with sails such as the one pictured here.

found in other parts of the world, including the Indian swamp deer, the Blue Bull of Nilgai, and the four-horned antelope. There are also magnificent Bengal tigers and rare snow leopards, and in the forests live bears, panthers, wolves, monkeys and snakes.

To the north of India lie the countries of Nepal and Tibet, two of the highest countries in the world. Mt. Everest, the highest peak in the world, is in Nepal. Most of the people in this region live on the lower slopes of the Himalayas, where valleys are fertile and green and crops such as rice, maize and wheat are grown. Tibet is a small Buddhist country with the sacred city of Lhasa as its capital. Before the Chinese occupied Tibet in 1950, nearly one man in five was a Buddhist monk.

South-east Asia is the area to the east of India and south of China, and it includes many of the smaller countries on the mainland—Thailand, Laos, Cambodia and North and South Vietnam—as well as the island countries in the East Indies— Malaysia, Indonesia and the Philippines.

South-east Asia's climate is semi-tropical to tropical, and the countries in this area produce such goods as rice, tea, maize, rubber, and coffee for the rest of the world. It was in this part of the world that one of the most violent volcanic eruptions took place when the island of Krakatoa exploded in 1883. Debris from Krakatoa was carried on the ocean for hundreds of miles, and the sound of the blast was heard 3,000 miles away in South Australia. Mammoth ocean waves were produced, some of which affected seas as far away as the English Channel!

China is the largest country in Asia and in population the largest in the world. It is for the most part an agricultural country, and since the Revolution in the late 1940's when the communists came into power, farms have been organized as communes. Communes are not owned by one man but are worked by groups of families who share out what they produce. Rice is the main food of the Chinese, and crops such as maize, wheat, barley and millet are grown in the North. Tea is grown in the western and southern parts of the country. China is also rich in minerals, including deposits of high quality coal.

Since China is so big, a great effort has been made to improve railways, roads, and air travel so that people may go from one part of the country to another more easily. The Chinese have also made use of

89

the country's rivers and canal systems—there are now over 100,000 miles of inland waterways in China, or over twice as many as there were in 1949 when the communists took power.

Only two foreign territories remain on the Chinese mainland—Macao, which belongs to Portugal, and Hong Kong, a British Crown Colony. Because of her good position on the trade routes, Hong Kong has become a great trading centre and is a stopping-off point for passenger and cargo ships and aircraft.

Japan, situated on a group of islands, is off the east coast of mainland Asia. The four main islands are Honshu, Shikoku, Kyushu and Hokkaido; the capital city, Tokyo, is on Honshu. Less than half of Japan's people work the land, and more and more Japanese are moving to the cities where there are more jobs and they can earn more money. Since Japan has a mountainous landscape, farming must be done on the hillsides. The Japanese have carved

terraces in the hills, on which they grow crops such as rice, wheat and barley.

To add to their food supply, the Japanese have for centuries turned to the sea, and fish is still an important part of the Japanese diet. In addition to fishing just off shore, Japanese fishing fleets go to the north Pacific to catch salmon and crabs and to the Antarctic Ocean to catch whales. Japan is also the leading shipbuilding nation in the world, and produces the world's largest ships, especially oil-tankers.

Traditional Japanese life has become much more Westernized in recent years, and Japan's large cities look no different from large cities in Europe or America. Visitors to Japan often remark on the simple and attractive designs used in decorating Japanese houses and in arranging gardens. This love for simple and perfect designs is one of the Japanese traditions that has remained despite Western influences. The art of flower arrangement and the formal Tea Ceremony

Buddhist temples such as this one at Nikko are beautiful examples of the traditional architecture of Japan.

are two other traditions that have influenced modern Japanese design and are still carried on.

The high quality of Japanese design carries over into the area of manufacturing as well. There are few parts of the world that are not familiar with Japanese products such as cars, sewing-machines and transistor radios, which are well-designed, efficiently produced, and which often cost less than those produced elsewhere.

A Japanese actor in his colourful lion costume in the traditional butterfly and lion dance.

A Japanese family out for a walk. The wife and baby are in traditional costume; the husband is in a European suit. At home he changes to Japanese clothes.

Insects

There are in the world today enormous numbers of insects; in fact, well over three-quarters of all living creatures are insects. In many ways these tiny creatures help man. Without insects many of our garden vegetables and flowers would not grow. Also, they serve as food for many animals who would otherwise eat foods useful to man. In a few countries insects are eaten as food by people who consider them great delicacies.

The tiniest of all insects—a pygmy wasp—could wriggle easily through the eye of an ordinary sewing-needle. Side by side with this midget the common two-spot ladybird looks like a giant. Yet dozens of ladybirds would be needed to equal the bulk of the European stag-beetle; and this, again, seems quite tiny when compared

Tropical ants can stitch leaves together using silk-spinning grubs.

with its big relations from other countries, such as the Goliath beetles of West Africa, and the elephant beetles of tropical South America. The most amazing of these monsters is the so-called Hercules beetle, which may measure as much as six inches from end to end.

Very strange insects are the lantern-flies; they have enormous hollow projections from the front of their heads, like ridiculous noses. These nebs or beaks were formerly thought to give off light, but this has been proven untrue. The real "fire-flies" are certain beetles of which the British glow-worm is the best-known example. Much larger and more brilliant is a member of the skip-jack tribe, common in Brazil, where it goes by the name "cucuju". It has a pair of polished circular patches, one on each side of the thorax—the section of the body immediately behind the head—and one underneath its tail-

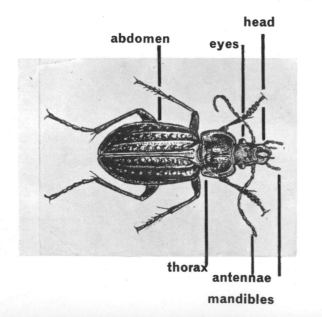

abdomen   eyes   head   thorax   antennae   mandibles

end, all three of which shine brightly at night.

Some of the lantern-flies referred to above are supposed to use their "beaks" for leaping, by striking them suddenly against the ground or the branch on which they are sitting, and so hurling themselves into the air when danger threatens, like the familiar frog-hopper. But in the case of one tropical American insect, known as the alligator-bug, the huge, hollow projection from the front of the head serves quite a different purpose. If seen from one side it conveys the impression of a tiny alligator's snout. The real eye is situated far back. We can hardly doubt that by means of this fierce-looking face this extraordinary insect is protected from the attacks of its enemies.

All normal adult insects have six jointed legs. The hind legs of most grasshoppers are very long and operated by powerful muscles, enabling these insects to make the astonishing leaps for which they are famous. The fore-legs of other insects are specially made for capturing and holding prey. Those of the giant fish-killing bugs of Central and South America

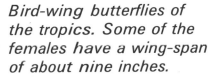

Bird-wing butterflies of the tropics. Some of the females have a wing-span of about nine inches.

end in a single sharp claw, and fold up under the head like a clasp-knife when not in use. But the most terrifying fore-legs are those of the praying mantis. They have dreadful-looking spiky limbs with which these fierce-looking and greedy creatures snatch at and grasp their prey.

The South American harlequin beetle spends most of its time climbing trees, and its very long fore-legs—like the arms of a spider monkey—enable it to reach upward and pull itself from one branch to another. The limbs of the daddy long-legs may seem to be much too large for its thin body and of little use to their owner, but in fact they are used for hanging on to blades of grass when the insect is in its natural surroundings. It only wanders into houses by accident. The middle- and hind-legs of water beetles and bugs are used for swimming, and are usually more or less shaped like oars or paddles. But no one has so far been able to explain why the long hind-legs of some tropical American plant-bugs are decorated with flag-like additions.

The sense organs of insects, especially the eyes and the antennae, are wonderfully planned. Many adult insects have two sorts of eyes—a large compound eye on each side of the head and a few smaller simple eyes, called "ocelli", on the brow. The latter are used not only to distinguish between light and darkness, but for seeing the pattern of light in the sky, by means of which they find their way about. Bees, for example, find their way home in this way. The large eyes are called compound because they consist of numerous parts—as many as 27,000 in the case of some moths—each of which is something like the lens of a camera. It has been suggested that the difference between the way human beings see and the way insects see is roughly the same as the difference between looking through a sheet of plate glass and looking through a diamond-leaded window. Because of this, insects are quicker to spot movement in their field of vision.

As far as eyes are concerned, the stalk-eyed flies of tropical Asia and Africa rank among the oddest of all insects. As their name implies, their eyes—as well as their tiny antennae—are placed at the end of two stalks that stand out like long horns.

The antennae of insects vary greatly in appearance and the purposes they serve. Ants and some other insects seem to recognize each other by rubbing or tapping one another's antennae. In most cases, however, these organs appear to play the part of the nose, and sometimes the ears too, in which case the "ears" are found at the base of the antennae. But in most insects the organs of hearing are located on some other part of the body. The beautiful feathered antennae of certain male moths and those of chafer beetles serve to expose to the atmosphere as large a surface as possible, in order to pick up particles of scent and pass the impulses these create to the nerve-centres. But the antennae of some insects—such as those of the Timberman beetle, which are five times as long as its body—are puzzling. Nobody has so far been able to tell us what they are used for.

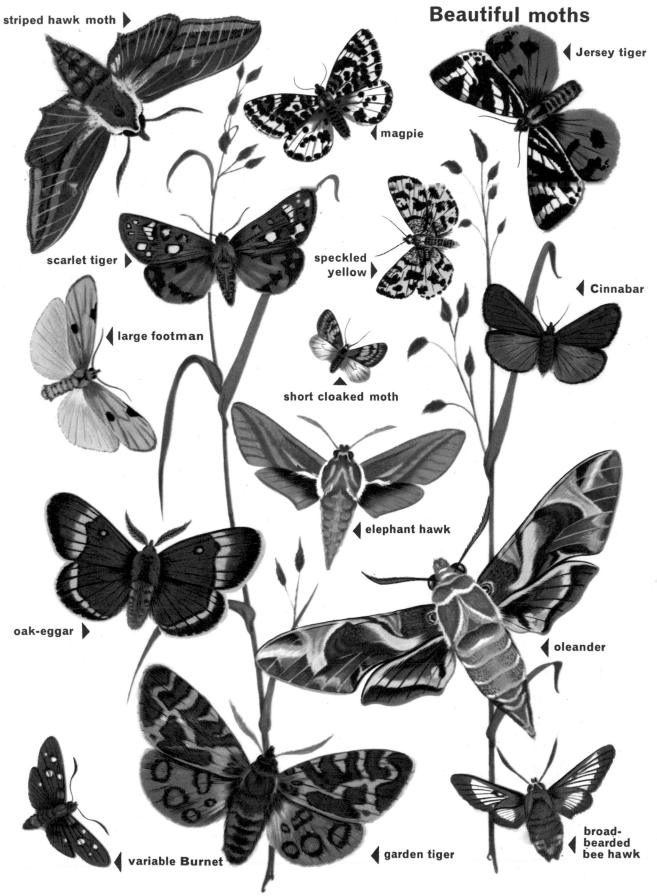

striped hawk moth ▶

Beautiful moths

◀ Jersey tiger

◀ magpie

scarlet tiger ▶

speckled yellow

◀ Cinnabar

large footman ◀

short cloaked moth ▲

◀ elephant hawk

oak-eggar ▶

◀ oleander

◀ variable Burnet

garden tiger ◀

broad-bearded bee hawk

Mammals

In the animal kingdom, mammals are the group of warm-blooded animals, including man, which bear their young alive and feed them with milk. The word mammal comes from the Latin *mamma*, meaning breast, for all mammals have glands that produce milk on which their offspring feed.

Another important thing about mammals is that in nearly every case they have an outer covering of hair. Mammals are vertebrates; that is, they have a backbone, also they breathe air through lungs. Whales, which are mammals and not fishes, must come to the surface every so often to take in lungfuls of air. Mammals have two pairs of limbs, but in some cases these have changed their normal form. Whales, for example, have flukes instead of hind limbs to help them in the water. Bats, too, have changed their front

The jerboa, or kangaroo rat, is a native of the North American desert. Like a kangaroo, this creature sits up on its hind legs and can leap 6 to 8 feet at a time.

The common mole lives underground and is an export digger. With the strong claws on its front paws it can hollow a tunnel out at the rate of fifteen feet an hour.

limbs into a kind of wing that enables them to fly.

In mammals the senses of smell, taste, sight, touch and hearing are very sharp, but never all equally so. Sometimes one sense is sharper to make up for another that is not; for example, the mole is nearly blind but has a most sensitive nose. The big-eared jerboa has very large ears and hence a most acute sense of hearing. Perhaps the most advanced sense in mammals is that of sight. The cats are good hunters because of their very keen eyesight, although they can also track by smell. It should be noted, however, that the vision of most mammals is one-coloured; that is, they see only a greyish world about them. The exceptions are the apes, who can see the same colours we can.

The colour of the coat of many mammals is a form of camouflage, or disguise, to protect them from attacks by other animals or, in the case of the cats, to hide them when they are hunting. A good ex-ample of this is the striking pattern of the leopard, which makes the animal most difficult to see by its prey when it is hunting. The camouflage colour of some animals changes with the seasons; for example, the fur of the ermine is white in the winter to blend with its snowy surroundings, but in the summer it changes to a brownish colour.

Mammals eat a wide variety of foods and are usually specially suited to their diet. For example, the long neck of the giraffe allows it to get at the high green foliage of the trees; the tiger's powerful teeth and jaws are ideal for tearing and eating flesh. The giant ant-eater is toothless but has a long, sticky tongue with which it can lick up the ants and termites on which it feeds; it also has powerful claws with which to tear open termites' nests.

All mammals bear their young alive with the exception of a few primitive mammals like the platypus, which lays

97

The three-toed sloth is a strange animal. It spends most of its life hanging upside-down by its long hooked claws. When it is awake it spends its time eating leaves or wild fruits.

The ibex, a wild goat once common to the Alps, has now almost disappeared.

eggs. As parents mammals are as careful as human beings. The lioness is an excellent parent, not only in watching over her cubs but, when they are old enough, teaching them the skills of hunting for prey. So great is the concern of most mammals to care for and protect their families that even the most gentle creature will attack when its young are threatened.

Mammals are a varied lot. Some of the shrews and mice are tiny, weighing several to the ounce. The African elephant is the biggest creature that lives on land, but at only five or six tons it is very small when compared with the whales. These big whales can live only in the water, which supports them evenly. They are so bulky that they collapse and die if stranded on the shore. But, like all other mammals, they have to use lungs and their young, born alive, feed on their mothers' milk.

The mammals include most of the

The hippopotamus, whose name means ''river-horse'', is one of the largest mammals. It spends most of its time in the water, feeding on aquatic plants.

The elephant is the largest of the land mammals; it lives in Africa and Asia, and feeds on plants, which it gathers with its long trunk.

animals which produce our food and clothing, and, oddly enough, most of these belong to one small group—the ones that chew the cud. They are the cow, sheep and goat, the yak, camel, llama, and reindeer. Cud-chewing animals have complicated stomachs which allow them to swallow mouthfuls of greenstuff and chew it over later at their leisure. When you next see a herd of cows taking their ease, watch one of them very carefully as it chews. After perhaps a minute of peaceful chewing it

swallows the mouthful; then, almost immediately, a little lump can be seen rippling up the throat to the mouth. When this has been chewed properly it is sent down to that part of the stomach where digestion takes place and another bit of unchewed, undigested food is sent up.

Other mammals have different ways of carrying the food away to eat it later in safety. Some of the monkeys, especially the African kind, have cheek pouches into which they can stuff so much food that

The male Mountain Gorilla may be up to 65 inches tall, weigh 500 lb., and have an armspread of 8 feet. It lives in the mountains east of the Congo.

The tiger, a member of the cat family, depends on its protective colouring, speed and stealthy attack for catching its prey. Tigers are native to India and the Far East.

their faces become unrecognizable. So have many of the rodents, or gnawing animals, including the well-known hamster.

Many mammals are wonderfully suited to the climates in which they must live. Some of the best examples are those animals that live in the desert, for water in a desert is often desperately short, and desperate measures must be used by animals living there to avoid being dried up or dying of thirst. One of the most interesting of the desert mammals is the kangaroo-rat of the deserts of the south-west U.S.A. This little creature sleeps underground in a burrow by day, and so escapes the sun's heat. Kangaroo-rats kept in captivity have been known to live for long periods, without drinking, on a diet of dry seeds. The amount of water in these seeds is very small, though there is more than one might

Mammals of the Sea: *From left to right; walrus, right whale, sea lion, porpoise. In the background a sperm-whale spouts vapour into the air. Like land mammals, all these animals bear live young which feed on their mothers' milk.*

102

think, and the kangaroo-rat's body does not waste a bit. It has no sweat-glands, and any moisture in the breath is condensed inside the nostrils and passes back into the body to be used again.

Very few of the animals living in deserts have been as thoroughly studied as the kangaroo-rat, but we may be sure that many of them save water in much the same ways. There are, however, some large desert animals. One of them, the Arabian oryx, a large antelope about the size of a pony, has been watched for 60 days during which time it was not seen to drink. Apparently it gets its water by eating desert plants that store water in their stems.

The mammals that are most like man are, of course, the ape family. They include the gibbons, orang-utans, chimpanzees and gorillas. They differ from all other monkeys in having no tail. They also have very long arms, used for swinging through the trees, and when walking on the ground the weight of the body is taken by the flat of the foot. The largest of the apes is the gorilla, of West and Central Africa. The gorilla may reach a height of six feet and weigh 450 pounds. Gorillas keep to the ground, wandering in family parties in search of fruit and other plant foods; at night they sleep in temporary litters of branches and leaves, either in forks low in the trees or on the ground between the roots, but in a new litter each night.

There is hardly a region of the world that has not been populated by the mammals, from the freezing arctic to the dense tropical jungles. Mammals of the sea include others besides whales. Members of the dolphin family are mammals, and are known either as dolphins or porpoises, although some are called whales. This is somewhat confusing. The largest of the dolphin family, for example, is the large killer whale, the only whale to prey on other warm-blooded animals. Other sea mammals include seals, walruses and the sea otter of the North Pacific.

The Rosetta Stone, which was discovered in Egypt in 1799, is inscribed in three languages, including Greek. It provided scholars with the key to understanding Egyptian hieroglyphics.

Our World Long Ago

A long time before writing was invented the world was inhabited by people who lived in houses and cities much as we do, and who did all sorts of interesting things. Unfortunately, nearly all their buildings became ruins and fell to the ground many centuries ago. They were gradually buried in sand and dust, blown over them by the wind. Perhaps the most exciting discoveries of all are those of the men who have dug deep down into the earth in order to uncover the remains of towns and cities built by people who lived thousands of years ago.

The remains of one of the oldest civilizations of all are in Egypt, where the great pyramids were already ancient monuments by the time proper writing was invented. The pyramids are the tombs of kings, but the people of ancient Egypt built massive tombs not only for their kings and queens, but also for important officers of state. Only a few stand above ground like the pyramids; most of them were cut into the hard rock below the ground, or into the side of a hill. The archaeologists who are looking for them can sometimes tell where they are by the shape of the surface of the ground, a change in the colour of the soil, or even by the presence of weeds which have very long roots.

The contents of such a tomb vary according to the importance of the person buried, but the ancient Egyptians were a religious people who believed that the dead pass on to another world, and they took care to provide them with the things they thought necessary for the journey. These might include furniture, vessels of pottery, food, jewels and weapons. The body itself was preserved and wrapped in cloth to make a "mummy", and this was sometimes decorated with jewels or wore a necklace

In 1922, Lord Carnarvon and Howard Carter made one of the greatest discoveries of all time when they uncovered Tutankhamun's tomb in Egypt.

The Parthenon, an ancient Greek temple to the goddess Athena, is one of the most beautiful ancient buildings in the world.

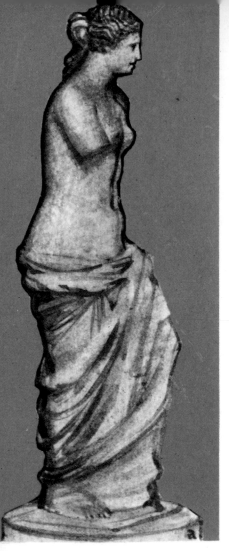

The famous Greek statue of the "Venus de Milo" got its name from the island of Milos, where it was discovered.

and rings. The richest tombs were naturally those of the kings, and most of the great kings or "pharaohs" of Egypt were buried near each other in the "Valley of the Kings", an area about 350 miles south of the pyramids.

In Greece, many of the famous temples, theatres, markets and other public buildings of the ancient Greeks have been uncovered and sometimes partly restored. Fallen pillars have been set upright once more, and even parts of buildings have been reconstructed. In this way we may get an idea of what the buildings we read of in the classics really looked like. Much of ancient Athens has been restored in this way, and today the great temple of the Parthenon looks, from a distance, much like it did when it was first built.

An interesting example of a city that has been wonderfully preserved from the

A human figure in lava and volcanic ash was discovered, still preserved, in the ruins of Pompeii after nearly 2000 years.

past is Pompeii, in southern Italy. Situated at the foot of the volcano, Vesuvius, Pompeii was at one time a busy city, until disaster struck (A.D. 79): Vesuvius erupted and buried Pompeii under layers of cinders and ashes. For years this great city lay buried beneath the surface of the earth, but it was finally discovered and dug out. Now visitors can see its ruins, which are almost perfectly preserved, and which show us just what an ancient Roman city was like.

Far away from Pompeii, the remains of the great civilizations of the Mayas and the Aztecs of Central America have been uncovered. From them we have learned a great deal about these people who were related to the Indians of North America, and who were skilled craftsmen and artists. They built huge temples very much like the pyramids of Egypt, but many of them were destroyed by the Spanish conquerors in the 16th century. The Great Pyramid of the Sun in Mexico, which may still be seen, measures nearly 230 yards along each side at its base, and rises to a flat top 200 feet high. In the Mayan cities the streets and court-yards were paved with cement, and they had drainage systems which ran underneath their buildings. In fact, in many ways the Mayas were as advanced as the ancient Greeks, and were not, by any means, a "primitive" civilization!

An artist's idea of what one of the temples of the ancient Aztecs looked like before they were ruined and became covered in jungle growth.

The Plant World

Most of the plants in our world live partly above ground and partly below. The parts above the ground are the stem and its branches, and the leaves and flowers. The parts below, which are not usually seen, are the roots.

Many flowering plants can only multiply if they are pollinated, and to do this they need the help of insects. If you pull a petal carefully off a flower, you may see a tiny pocket at the end where it was joined. In this pocket lies nectar, a sweet substance made by the flower to attract bees. A number of other kinds of flowers have these pockets of nectar, and others, in addition, may be scented or brightly coloured so as to make them more attractive to their visitors. When a bee settles on the flower to collect its nectar, it brushes some of the flower's pollen onto the "pistil", the part of the flower which, when pollinated, will form the seeds for new plants.

Some flowers, like those of the grasses and those on hazel and birch trees, rely upon the wind to do the same work as the bee. This is a much less certain method of pollination because the wind may scatter the pollen too much. Such flowers have to produce their pollen, or "dust", in great quantities. Incidentally, we mentioned grasses as being flowers. It is true they look very different from most kinds of flowers we know, but nevertheless they are flowering plants just the same, and are very successful ones at that. It is just that over a long period of time changes have taken place that have altered the flower so that a grass in bloom does not look like other flowers.

Usually when we speak of trees we mean tall woody plants with a single main trunk and bearing branches covered with leaves. Strangely enough, however, there is no real scientific difference between small plants (which we usually call herbs), shrubs and trees, for there are some herbs that develop woody stems and some shrubs may have quite thick trunks. But we may separate shrubs and herbs from trees by their difference in size. Trees usually live for many years and thickened tissue (wood) grows in the form of rings, which can be seen on the stump or cut end of a felled trunk.

"Coniferous", or cone-bearing trees like pines and firs, are found in the colder climates, and are generally green all year round. "Deciduous" trees, those that shed their leaves each year, occur further south.

Conifer trees from the vast forests of Canada provide over half the world's wood pulp, used in making newsprint and paper.

Some trees yield other products. The first of such trees that comes to mind is the rubber tree, the growing of which is a major industry in Ceylon, Malaya, and Indonesia. Another important tree is the coconut palm, common in tropical and semi-tropical regions of the world. Its wood is used for building, its leaves for thatching, and the coconut itself as food and for the oil it produces.

Many trees other than the coconut palm provide us with nuts. These include the Brazil nut, the cashew nut, the butter nut and the cola nut, to mention just a few. Other trees are the source of many useful products. There is the cork oak, which provides us with cork, the cinchona tree, yielding quinine, and trees which give off gums and resins.

Of all the hardwoods of the temperate forests none is so well known as the oak. It is justly called the "king of the forest" because of its slow growth and stately bearing. It has been used in the past, and is still valuable today, in all work that requires great strength and wearing power. Many a building has been built with sturdy beams of oak, including some fine old churches, halls, barns, and cottages. It was extensively used in shipbuilding in the days of sail. Elm wood, used for gunwales of boats, in farm building, for making wheel-barrows and for hubs in cart-wheels, is another well known hardwood, as are walnut, beech, sycamore, and hornbeam.

Giant redwoods

1 Traveller's Joy (flower)
2 Dog Rose
3 Foxglove
4 Hemlock
5 Traveller's Joy (seeded)
6 Brome Grass
7 Wild Teasel

8 Honeysuckle
9 Bryony
10 Wood Anemone
11 Ladies Smock
12 Ox-eyed Daisy
13 Field Poppy
14 Chicory

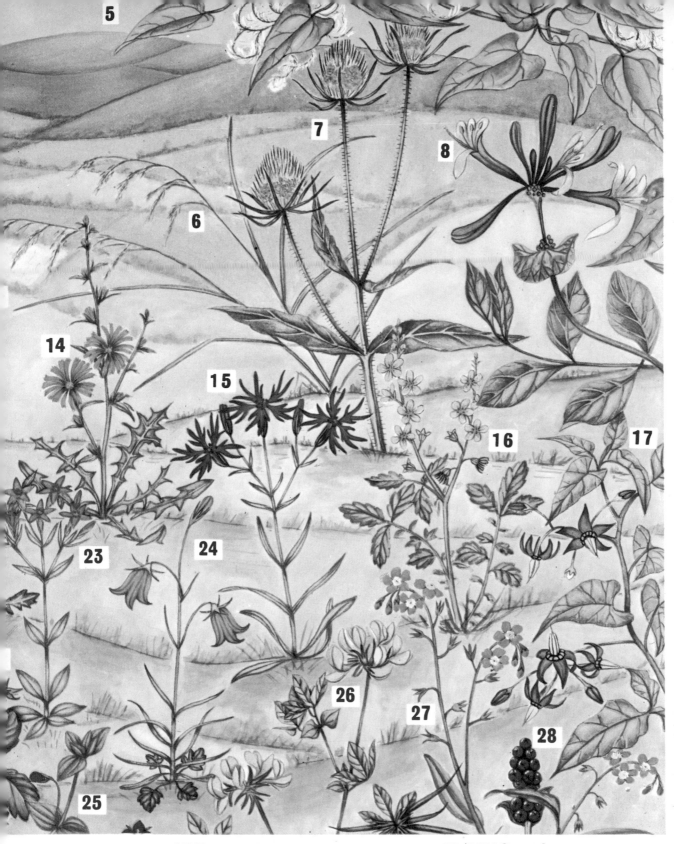

15 Ragged Robin
16 Agrimony
17 Woody Nightshade
18 Coltsfoot
19 Cuckoo-pint (flower)
20 Celandine
21 Bugle

22 Wild Strawberry
23 Centaury
24 Harebell
25 Scarlet Pimpernel
26 Bird's Foot Trefoil
27 Forget-me-not
28 Cuckoo-pint (fruit)

The Polar Regions

A view taken from the air of the snowy mountains in Baffin Land, an Arctic island off Labrador.

The Arctic region of the world is the cold, icy area around the North Pole. On a globe the Arctic Circle is marked at 66° 30′ N. though the Arctic really has no exact boundary. It is north of the "tree line", that is, the line beyond which very few trees grow. Parts of northern Canada, Alaska, Russia, Scandinavia and most of Greenland are within the Arctic Circle.

In the summer, the southern parts of the Arctic are covered with low plants and are quite green, but in the winter the land is covered with ice and snow, and the Arctic seas freeze over. It is bitterly cold and for days at a time temperatures often stay many degrees below 0° F.

One of the earliest explorers of the Arctic regions was Eric the Red, who lived about 980 A.D. He sailed across the Atlantic from Scandinavia to Greenland, where he started a colony. After Eric many Norsemen sailed into Arctic waters, but no other Europeans tried to do this until the early 16th century, when explorers began searching for a route to China through the New World. One of the

Adélie penguins on the rocky edge of the land overlooking pack ice and icebergs.

first of these daring men was Sebastian Cabot, who led an expedition sometime around 1538. The riches of the East encouraged others to try and find the shortest route to China, and in 1576 Sir Martin Frobisher led an expedition to find a north-west passage from the Atlantic to the Pacific Ocean. Since that time, many men have faced the dangers of the Arctic to find new trade routes or plot its geography. Some of the most famous of these men are Captain J. Ross (1819), Lieutenant J. Franklin (1818), Lieutenant E. Parry (1818), A. E. Nordenskiold (1868), Robert Peary (1886), Dr. Nansen (1888), Roald Amundsen (1903), and Commander R. E. Byrd, who flew over the North Pole in 1926. As recently as 1958, a different kind of exploration took place when the U.S.S. *Nautilus*, an atomic-powered submarine, made a voyage under the Arctic ice cap to try and find new and faster routes for cargo ships through the frozen seas.

Eskimos are native to the Arctic regions. They have learnt to provide food, clothing and shelter for themselves and until recently were able to live very full and free lives despite the hardships of Arctic life. They are expert hunters with the harpoon, which they use to kill such Arctic animals as polar bears, walruses, and seals. These animals provide them not only with meat but with almost everything else they need. They use animal skins for their clothing and the fur to line their outer coats, or "parkas". They sharpen fish and animal bones into needles, knives and other tools. Whale oil and animal fats are used to light lamps, and Eskimo children think whale blubber makes a delicious sweet! Since they have no building materials such as wood or brick, some Eskimos use the material they have the most of—ice—

An Eskimo drying skins which will be traded for such household necessities as sugar, flour, tinned meats and oils.

to build their winter homes. They chop the ice into blocks and build them up into a small dome-shaped houses called igloos. Inside these ice houses it is snug and warm and Eskimos can even build a fire indoors without melting the roof!

In recent years the Eskimos have been in much closer contact with Europeans and their old ways of life are quickly disappearing. Their increasing contact with non-Eskimos has come about partly because several nations have built early-warning defence systems in the Arctic to guard against surprise missile attacks.

The Antarctic region of the world is the area around the South Pole spreading northward as far as the 60° southern parallel. The Antarctic has no trees and little plant life of any kind. The only animals that are able to survive in the Antarctic are fish-eaters like penguins, skua gulls, whales, and seals. One of the most interesting creatures and one of nature's funniest is the Emperor penguin, which is the largest bird in the penguin family. In their white shirts and dinner jackets the Emperors are funny creatures to watch. They greet one another with little bows, and walk over the ice either upright or on their bellies, kicking with their feet. The Adélie penguin, smaller than the Emperor, is also playful. Adélies often take "joy-rides" on pieces of floating ice, and once a group of them even hitched a ride on a submarine that was cruising through Antarctic waters!

Antarctic exploration did not begin until the 1700's. One of the first men to set sail for this forbidding land was Captain James Cook, who led an expedition in 1772. Others who made important voyages to the Antarctic were Fabian von Bellingshausen (1819), James Weddell (1823), John Bisco (1830), Jules Dumont d'Urville (1840), Charles Wilkes (1839), J. Clark Ross (1840), Roald Amundsen (1901), Captain R. F. Scott (1901), and Sir Ernest Shackleton (1901).

About ten years ago many of the nations of the world got together and decided to make 1957—58 a year for studying the physical nature of the earth. One of the areas they decided to study was the Antarctic, since little was known at that time about this region. The scientific work they did included studies of the weather, to see how it might affect the rest of the world, the flow of sea currents, plant life, mineral deposits, and sea life. The work was not easy, for the scientists had to battle the constant cold that froze the equipment and the men as well. As part of the study, Dr. Vivian Fuchs led yet another exploring expedition across the frozen continent from Shackleton Base to Scott Base on the Ross Sea. Half-way across he met a New Zealand party led by the famous mountaineer, Sir Edmund Hillary, who climbed Mt. Everest in 1953. In addition to dog sleds the party used "snocars"—caravan-like vehicles that have caterpillar wheels for travelling over ice and snow.

Many research stations in the Antarctic are still active in carrying on scientific projects, for we have only just begun to learn about this forgotten part of the world.

A cliff of solid ice in Antarctica. It was over this kind of land that Sir Edmund Hillary battled to meet Sir Vivien Fuchs on their celebrated journey in 1958.

A scientific base in Antarctica. During the dark winter months the men stay inside their heated huts, coming out only to read their instruments or to feed their dogs.

Prehistoric Animals

The first living things existed perhaps 2,000 million years ago, and they lived in the sea, but they were too soft to be preserved in the rocks as fossils, so we have little way of knowing what they were actually like. From these minute creatures, during the next 1,500 million years or so, there came a good many other kinds of animals. There were corals, sea anemones, star fishes, crabs, shell-fish, and eventually the fishes themselves. It didn't happen as simply as that, though: it was a long and complicated story for which there is not room here.

Among the river fishes, however, were a few that could breathe air. These lung breathers were very much like a fish that has recently been caught in the sea off Madagascar, a "Coelacanth". Some of these fishes left the river bed and came to live on the land; they became the first land animals.

From these fishes there developed a new kind of animal, an amphibian. It gets its name because, like the air-breathing fishes, it could live on the land or in the water. Frogs, toads, and newts are amphibians that exist today, but the first amphibians were large, awkward creatures, sometimes six or seven feet long, crawling on all fours.

For thousands of years these great animals of the swamps were the largest and most advanced animals on the face of the earth, but after a time one kind of amphibian gave rise to an even more advanced kind of creature—a reptile. When you think of the reptiles of the present time, the snakes and tortoises, the crocodiles and the lizards, this will not seem a great advance, but the reptiles of the past were much more important and very much more exciting.

The first reptiles, it is true, were as awkward and as sprawling as the great amphibians. But they were able, being reptiles, to lay their eggs on the land, and though they were cold-blooded, as all reptiles are even today, they were able to run about on the land with some speed, as the climate was warmer than it is now. For more than 100 million years they were masters of the world.

After a period on the land some of them took once more to the sea, the most important ones being the Plesiosaurs and the Ichthyosaurs. Both of these were largish animals, some being as much as thirty feet long. Both kinds had paddle-like legs, which the Plesiosaurs used entirely for swimming, actually rowing themselves over the sea. The Ichthyosaurs, however, propelled themselves with a large tail fin like that of a fish, using their flippers for steering. The Ichthyosaurs were born alive; that is, the eggs were hatched in the body of the mother.

In the air above the earth other reptiles were flying. They were the Pterodactyls. Most of them were small—not much larger than the ordinary bird we see in our gardens—but they had no feathers and they had a scaly skin like other reptiles. This

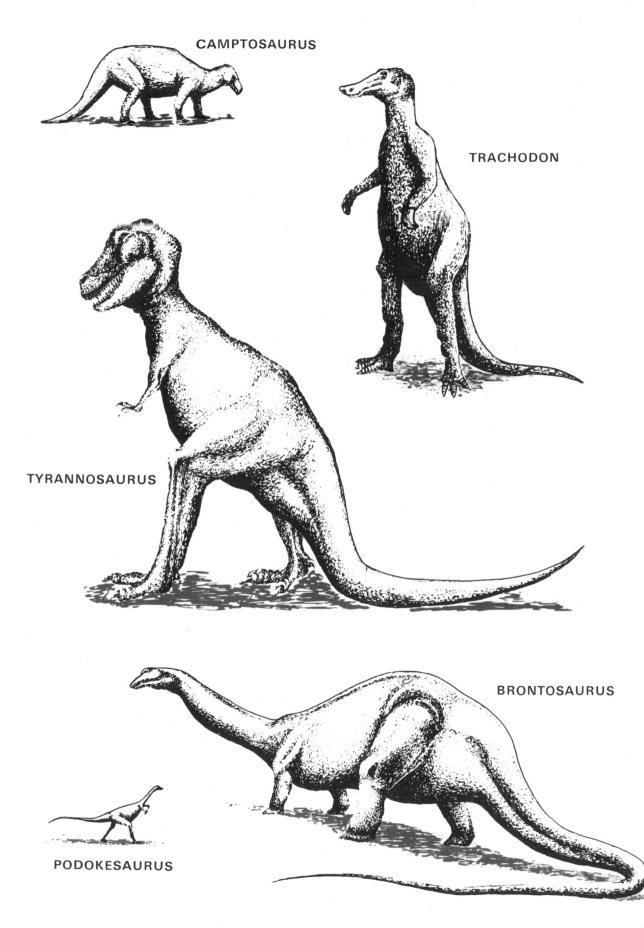

CAMPTOSAURUS

TRACHODON

TYRANNOSAURUS

BRONTOSAURUS

PODOKESAURUS

117

skin covered not only the body but made a web stretching from the side of the body and top of the hind leg to the hand. Some of the flying reptiles had tails, with a small tail fin, but most of them were tail-less. Towards the end of the "Age of Reptiles", some of the flying reptiles had a wing spread of as much as twenty-two feet or so.

The real prehistoric monsters were the huge reptiles that lived on land during this period, the dinosaurs. Some of the dinosaurs ran on their hind legs, which were strong, and used their long tails to help balance themselves. The front legs of this type of dinosaur were small and could only have been used in resting or when feeding on their prey. The fingers and toes had sharp, stout claws and the mouth had sharp teeth so that they must have been fierce animals in their hunt for food. Some of these flesh eaters were fairly small, six or seven feet from head to tail, but others were more than thirty feet, and some were as long as fifty feet, their heads alone measuring nearly five feet.

Even so, such giants were by no means the largest of the dinosaurs. Great skeletons have been found in many parts of the world that show some of the dinosaurs to have walked on all fours and to have been over sixty or seventy feet long. We know some of these skeletons fairly well and from them we can calculate the weight of the complete animals, some of which may have been as much as forty tons. Such animals were too heavy for much movement on the land and they lived most of their time in the waters of quiet rivers, lakes or lagoons. Here the buoyancy of the water helped them to carry their weight and the animals roamed around eating up the vegetation that grew on the banks. They had the additional advantage that in the water the flesh-eaters could rarely get at them.

There were also vegetarian dinosaurs that lived on the land, and which must often have been pursued by their fierce neighbours. Some of these plant eaters also stood on their hind legs, and were probably able to run with some speed. Other vegetarian dinosaurs had even better protection, for though they lived on land and walked slowly on all fours, they had great spines and spikes, plates of bone and other "armour" on their backs, so that they must have looked like giant bony armadillos.

When the great reptiles became extinct, the smaller mammals, the little rat-like hairy creatures that did not lay eggs but also bore their young alive, had a better chance of survival. Soon the mammals took the place of the reptiles. At first they, too, were odd-looking creatures, though not so large or odd as the dinosaurs. It was they who gave rise to the kinds of animals we are all familiar with— the oxen and horses, the elephants and the lions and tigers. Though many large mammals are strangers to Europe now and are only seen in zoos, at one time, not many thousands of years ago, there were lions and bears and, during the ice-age, mammoths, along with woolly rhinoceroses and giant deer.

IGUANODON

ANKYLOSAURUS

SCELIDOSAURUS

STRUTHIOMIMUS

STEGOSAURUS

TRICERATOPS

Railways

No one knows exactly who invented the first railway, but wooden and then iron rails had been used in mines as far back as the 16th and 17th centuries to run coal cars on. By 1825, 22 iron railways were in use in Britain. All were privately owned but one—the first public railway was a little $9\frac{1}{2}$-mile, horse-drawn tramway running from a wharf on the Thames at Wandsworth to Croydon in Surrey. After the Stockton and Darlington Railway was opened in 1825, the next important line to be built was the Liverpool and Manchester Railway, which was opened in 1830. The owner of the line had hoped to get 500 passengers a day; in five years half a million were being carried!

Britain's first railway stations were usually the inns or road-houses which had been stops in the stage-coach routes. In London in 1841, passengers for Brighton had to book their places on the train one day ahead at either the *Blue Boar* Inn, in

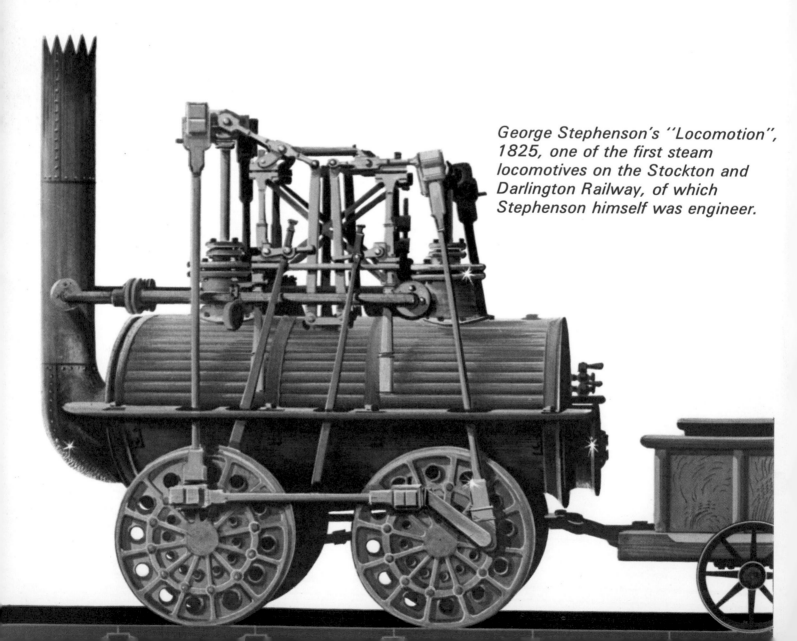

George Stephenson's "Locomotion", 1825, one of the first steam locomotives on the Stockton and Darlington Railway, of which Stephenson himself was engineer.

Holborn, or at the *Spread Eagle*, in Grace-church Street. Travelling by rail in those days was not nearly as comfortable as it is now. On the London and Birmingham Railways, for example, the third-class coaches carried four passengers on each side of coaches that had no roofs! Second-class passengers had a roof, but had to sit on bare board seats. The time the journey took depended upon which class train one travelled on, and travelling third class from London to Birmingham in the late 1830's took $3\frac{1}{2}$ hours longer than travelling first class!

There were many accidents in the early days of railways. Sometimes newly-made embankments collapsed under the weight of a train; sometimes wooden bridges or weak iron bridges gave way and the train plunged down on to a road or into a river. Often there were disasters when the couplings joining the coaches together snapped, since they were only chains loosely hooked together. Even just stopping and starting jolted the passengers tremendously, for there were no proper buffers between the cars so that they banged into one another constantly. Truly, anyone travelling by rail took his life in his hands!

In the early days, many railway accidents were also caused by the poor methods of signalling used. Lights were lit at stations to tell the driver if the track was clear, but if a train broke down in between stations, which often happened, the train behind it had no way of knowing and so very often there were tremendous collisions. The invention of the telegraph in

"Atlantic" type locomotive of the Great Northern Railway. This kind of engine was first introduced by H. A. Ivatt in 1898.

1837 helped to signal warnings, and nowadays, complicated mechanical signal systems make accidents almost impossible.

The first important British express train to be given a name was the famous *Flying Scotsman*, which has left King's Cross Station every day at 10 a.m. for just over a hundred years. Only four of the 80 titled expresses kept their names during the Second World War, when there was a disastrous set-back to the railways of Britain. These were the *Flying Scotsman*, the *Cornish Riviera, Limited Express*, the *Aberdonian*, and the *Night Scotsman*.

These days, railways are still being modernized. Steam locomotives are being replaced by diesel and electric engines; passenger trains are more roomy and soundproof and even freight trains are being run at express train speeds. Railway stations, which are so often dingy and cheerless, are slowly being replaced by brighter, cleaner buildings.

On the Continent of Europe, railways developed more slowly than in Britain. In France, in 1829, Marc Seguin constructed the first section of the railway line connecting the rivers Loire and Rhône from Givors to Rive-de-Gier. Six years later the line from Brussels to Malines was constructed, and in 1837 the French St. Germain line was finished. Today, the "Golden Arrow" ("Flèche d'Or") and the night-ferry express link Britain with the European continent, while Spain and Portugal are reached by way of the "Sud Express" which starts from Paris. Also from Paris, the "Simplon-Orient" express winds its way to Istanbul through Switzerland and the Simplon tunnel.

In Russia a railway track was laid from Leningrad to Pavlovsk in 1836, followed 12 years later by a railway line in Spain which stretched from Barcelona to Mataró, but the majority of European railways were not constructed until 1870.

A dramatic night scene showing the modern signals system that helps to keep the railways safe.

The South African Railways, which were started in 1867, today covers a route distance of 13,483 miles. There are two famous trains that cover vast distances on the African railways—the train which runs twice a week, travelling 999 miles from Cape Town via Kimberley and Johannesburg, and the "Orange Express" which makes the 1,099-mile journey to Durban twice weekly. Since the completion of the 838-mile Benguela railway in 1935, a traveller can now cross the continent from East to West entirely by rail, starting at the Port of Lobito and finishing at the Port of Beira, by way of Salisbury.

In Asia the start of Japan's 18,440 mile railway system began in 1872, but in spite of her late start, Japan today has one of the most modern railway systems in the world. The four main islands—Honshu, Kyushu, Hokkaido and Shikoku—are covered by a large railway network by which every important town and city can be reached by train. On the new Tokaido Line, which has trains running at 125 miles per hour, the Japanese have worked out a truly amazing safety system for controlling railroad traffic. Because the trains are going so fast, it is impossible for an engineer to recognize light signals in time to be able to stop. Instead, they have an automatic system by which the speed of a train is controlled according to its distance from the train in front of it. Special tracks slow down one train if it is getting too close to another, and if it is very close, the brakes are automatically applied. And if the automatic control system breaks down, electric signals are

An electric train running over the Landwasser Viaduct, on part of its journey through the towering mountains of Switzerland.

sent out which stop all the trains on the line automatically. It is certainly an almost foolproof system!

The government railway system in India was begun nineteen years earlier than Japan's, and today the line has a total of nearly 43,000 miles which cover the entire continent of Asia. Nowadays, a journey can be made from Bombay to Amritsar by way of the Northern Railway. The Punjab mail train from Victoria to

Bombay, a 1,196-mile journey, takes 29 hours. Burma and Thailand railways cover a distance of 2,000 miles, but the Asian country with the longest system of tracks is China, where railway lines stretch for 19,000 miles.

In Australia, it was 1854 when the first train began its run from Melbourne to the coast at Hobson's Bay (now Port Melbourne). Railways grew quickly, helping to open up the country and to carry the gold from the mines that were discovered inland to the coast.

Now Australia has several large railway companies to cover the country. Travelling across Australia on the Trans-Australian Railway is one of the most exciting journeys anywhere in the world.

Railways in America began in 1830 when Peter Cooper designed and built a

A diesel-electric train on its way across the Nullarbor Plain in Australia.

The "Aerotrain", a powerful modern long-distance train built by the American firm of General Motors.

little engine called *Tom Thumb*. Though several British engines had been tried earlier, this was the first American-made engine; it hauled 36 passengers at 18 miles per hour on the Baltimore and Ohio Railway at Baltimore, Maryland.

By the 1840's, cow-catchers, bells, chime whistles, "diamond" smoke-stacks and the engineman's cabin, or cab, were all familiar parts of American locomotives, and they became more and more unlike their English cousins. During the 1800's, railways became most important when the west was being settled, and the lines westward grew so quickly that by 1865 there were 33,000 miles of rail in the United States—almost twice the amount British

Railways can boast today, a century later! Riding on one of these trains presented the same dangers as did early trains elsewhere, but with a few added hazards— they were often attacked by Indians who were unhappy to have the "iron horses" steaming through their hunting grounds! The trains frightened away game, and the passengers considered it great sport to shoot at buffalo as they were riding along.

Today, however, American railway lines total 250,000 track miles, and American locomotives and coaches excel in comfort and size. The all-Pullman "Twentieth Century Limited" from New York to Chicago makes the 960-mile journey in 12 hours.

The rattlesnake, a native of the Americas, frightens its prey by shaking the rattle on the end of its tail.

Reptiles

Reptiles are cold-blooded backboned animals with bodies covered with scales. Their earliest known remains are found in some of the coal beds. At one time, between 150 and 70 million years ago, during the period known as the "Age of Reptiles", reptiles ruled the earth. There were, however, even then, crocodiles and tortoises, lizards and snakes. Many of the reptiles of that period have died out completely. One, the tuatara of New Zealand, is the sole survivor of its race. It is a living fossil.

The snake family is a large one, including about 2,000 different varieties. Snakes are limbless, although the pythons have the remains of hind limbs, including a pair of claws which are visible outside the skin. One important difference between snakes and lizards is that snakes have no movable eyelids. Their eyes are instead protected by a hard transparent covering.

Though many people believe that snakes "sting" with their tongues, this is not so. Snakes use their tongues the way we use our noses and ears, for they cannot hear and can only tell where they are and what is going on around them by using their eyes and "sniffing" with their tongues. Snakes that are hungry or annoyed will dart their tongues in and out more rapidly to "smell" better.

All snakes bite and the venom in the bite of a poisonous snake comes from its teeth and not from its tongue. These venomous snakes, like vipers and cobras, have special teeth, called fangs, which are hollow or grooved. The fangs work like a doctor's hypodermic needle. In vipers these fangs can be raised and powered by the action of the jawbones, which work like levers. The venom is made in special glands, and when the snake bites, these are squeezed so that the poison is forced down through the teeth and into the wound.

Snakes are able to swallow meals that are larger than their own heads because their jawbones are loose and the skin is very elastic. The halves of the lower jaw come apart at the tip and the bones that attach the jaw to the skull are movable, so that a snake can open its mouth tremendously wide.

Foods vary according to the size of the snake, and range from insects and worms to fair-sized pigs, small antelopes and birds. Some snakes do much good in destroying pests, and on many farms they are protected. The larger snakes kill their prey first by squeezing it to death. Such a monster as the thirty foot anaconda or python could easily crush a man, but it is doubtful whether it could swallow him. The boa constrictor, which many people believe can squeeze a man to death, is actually a much smaller snake, though it, too, squeezes its victims.

The largest living crocodile is the salt-water crocodile. It may be as much as 30 feet long. The smallest are the South

The snake has loosely-attached jaws which enable it to swallow whole animals that are larger than its own head.

American caimans. All live and feed mainly in water, often coming out on land to bask. There is little difference outwardly between a crocodile and an alligator. The one feature that distinguishes them is that in crocodiles the fourth tooth of the lower jaw fits into a notch in the side of the upper jaw, whereas in alligators this fourth tooth fits into a pit in the upper jaw. A crocodile, therefore, appears to have a permanent grin. The gharials are long-snouted crocodiles of India. Their jaws are more than usually slender and they have many teeth that lock together to hold the fish that form their food.

The largest tortoises are the giant tortoises of the Galapagos, with the shell some three feet long and the animal weighing about a quarter of a ton. The largest turtle is the luth or leathery turtle, up to eight feet long and weighing nearly a ton. No clear distinction can be made between tortoises and turtles, except that the first live on land and the second usually in water. No living tortoise or turtle has teeth, but its jaws are covered with a sharp, horny beak.

The most numerous reptiles today are the lizards, of which there are well over 2,000 different kinds, from the well-known slow-worm, the legless lizard of the countryside, to the Komodo dragon of the Indonesian islands, which grows to twelve feet long. Most of them feed on insects. Generally they are active, agile animals, although some, like the chameleons, specialize in moving slowly and stalking their prey. Because there are so many of them we can deal only with a few outstanding examples. Most lizards are quite harmless, seeking safety in swift flight. In this they are helped by their ability to throw off the greater part of the tail. There are, however, two poisonous lizards, the teeth of which are hooked and provided with poison glands.

The Komodo dragon, a powerful reptile of up to 12 feet long, lives on the island of Komodo, in Indonesia, where it feeds on wild pigs. It belongs to the animal family known as monitors.

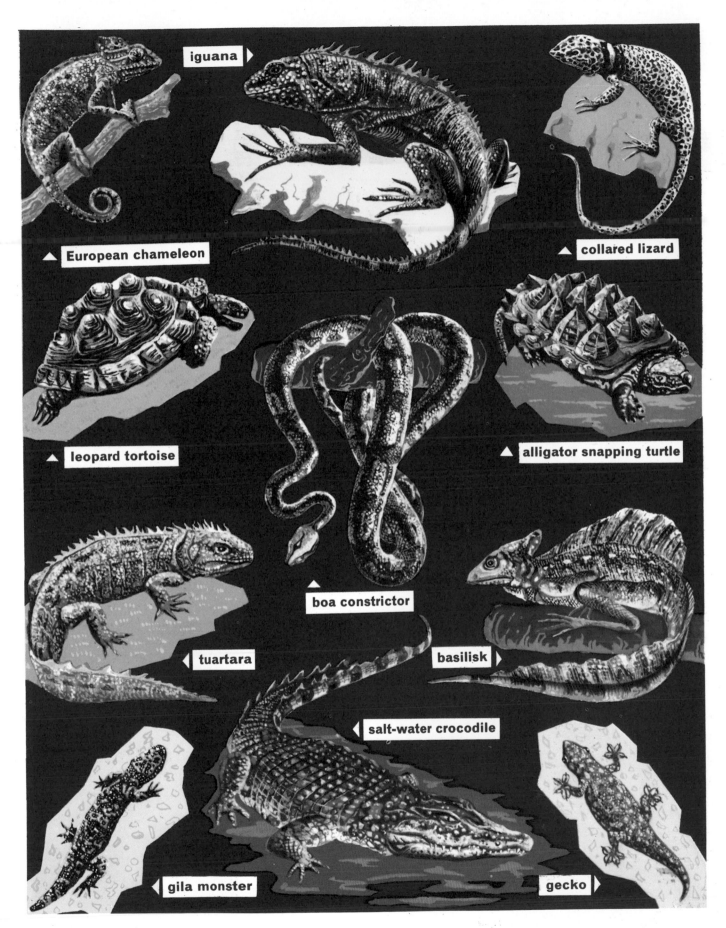

iguana

European chameleon

collared lizard

leopard tortoise

alligator snapping turtle

boa constrictor

tuartara

basilisk

salt-water crocodile

gila monster

gecko

Around 1500 B.C. Egyptians used trading vessels like this one to trade with people in the part of Africa that we now call Somaliland.

Ships

The first boats were made when primitive men carved out the trunks of trees into dugout canoes, which they rowed with their hands or with wooden paddles. Primitive tribes in Africa and South America still use this kind of boat. In places where trees didn't grow men made boats by tying lots of reeds together. The early Egyptians built the first real sea-going ships, which were wooden galleys with one sail that were driven through the water by long rows of oars. It was the Phoenicians who had the first strong navy. Their warships had two masts and often more than one bank of oars on each side. Sometimes they put metal caps on the high bows of their ships and used them as battering rams. The Greeks used very similar types of galleys for trading and as warships. They knew how to build good strong ships with well made keels and hulls.

When the Romans became more powerful than the Greeks they became masters of the seas. They built large galleys that were driven through the water by broad square sails, and high on the main masts were hoisted topsails. These ships were big enough to go right out into the ocean, and since the Romans used them to travel to the many lands they conquered, the ships helped the Roman Empire to become bigger and stronger.

After the fall of the Roman Empire it was the Vikings who ruled the seas. Their galleys or longboats could carry about two hundred men, and were driven by oar and sail. These ships could frighten the Viking's enemies, for often they carved ferocious-looking heads of serpents or dragons on the bows. The Vikings raided the lands around the Northern seas, and invaded England with 865 longboats. They also saw the New World long before Columbus did when they dared to take their ships across the Atlantic Ocean. A map that they drew showing part of Greenland, or "Vinland" as they called it, has recently been discovered.

Though galley ships got larger, they did not change much in other ways until the 10th century. Then, as trade grew, ships had to be bigger to carry more cargo and because of the threat of pirate attacks they also had to be faster. Oars were replaced by more sails. It was in this type of early sailing ship that Columbus crossed the Atlantic Ocean to the New World in 1492. When gunpowder was invented, ships were fitted with guns that loomed from the bows and upper decks. Forecastles and stern castles were built into these larger ships, now called galleons, to prepare them better for battle. War galleons didn't need space for cargo, so they were built with special gun decks strong enough to support big cannons. These big guns changed sea battles. No longer did two ships draw alongside each other to fight; instead they kept their distance so that they could fire their cannons. The *Ark Royal*, one of the sturdy

The Dutch used large vessels, called "East Indiamen" for trading with their colony in the East Indies. These ships could carry a great deal of cargo but were too bulky to move very fast and often fell prey to pirates.

The first clipper ships were designed and built in Baltimore, and
the designs were adopted by the British for ships going to the Far East.
A fully rigged clipper like this one probably carried a cargo of tea.

English ships that helped to defeat the Spanish Armada in 1588, weighed 800 tons and carried 55 guns.

During the 1600's trade on the high seas grew rapidly, and before long England and the other European countries were sending ships around the southern tip of Africa to trade with India and other lands in the East. The ships they used were made to hold cargo but were not very fast. Speed became more important as the competition for trade increased, so a new kind of ship, the clipper, was developed. Clipper ships were sleek, sharp-bowed vessels which were fast and very beautiful to look at as they skimmed over the water under full sail. The fastest clipper was probably the *Flying Cloud* which could cover over 370 sea miles a day on a good run. Another famous clipper was the *Cutty Sark*, which can still be seen at Greenwich, London.

In the early 1800's, at about the time when clipper ships were most popular, the first successful steam-powered ships appeared. The paddle steamer *Savannah* which went from New York to Liverpool in 1819, was the first steam-powered vessel to cross the Atlantic. However, paddlewheels were too slow for a man named Brunel, so in 1846 he designed the steamship *Great Britain* which used propellers instead of paddlewheels. As the steamships improved, they gradually took over the work of clipper ships.

Up until this time most people thought

One of the early paddle steamers, the Sirius, *started the first regular transatlantic service in 1838. Rigged like a sailing ship, she was 703 tons and carried 100 passengers on her first voyage.*

The Canberra, *one of the most up-to-date passenger liners, has a striking streamlined form with side-by-side funnels placed close to the stern.*

that it would be impossible to build an entire ship out of iron. They thought it would be too heavy to float well or to move very quickly. During the American Civil War, however, two ironclad warships that had been built just as an experiment, passed the test when they did battle with each other and proved that iron ships would work.

If ships were to be built of iron and steel, they needed stronger engines to drive them. Sir Charles Parsons invented one—a steam turbine engine—and in 1892 the diesel engine appeared, taking its name from the inventor, Rudolf Diesel. Instead of using steam for power, this engine uses oil.

Soon passenger ships were being built with turbine engines. The first Atlantic liner to use a turbine engine was the *Victorian*, a fast luxury ship that had a top speed of 19 knots. The *Lusitania*, one

Missile destroyers are rapidly being built by the world's leading navies. Some of the newer ones are atomic powered and carry guided missiles.

of the best known of these Atlantic "greyhounds", was sunk by a German submarine in 1915 with a loss of 1,198 lives.

Once it was proven that ships could be built with iron and steel it was not long before bigger and stronger warships appeared which could carry larger and more powerful guns. Typical examples of these naval dinosaurs were the French *Charles-Martel* (1893), which had steel plating 18-inches thick at the waterline,

and the German *Kaiser Barbarossa* (1900) which was heavily plated and just as heavily armed——she carried 38 guns and had five torpedo tubes.

During World War I battleships became even larger and carried even bigger and heavier guns. The British battleship *Hood*, one of the largest ships of her time, was finished just too late for the First World War, and was later sunk by the Germans during World War II. Submarines, which had been experimented with for many years, finally became accepted fighting vessels during World War I. During World War II submarines and aircraft became so good at destroying large battleships that aircraft carriers soon replaced battleships as the largest vessels in the navy. These were built so that bombers and other aircraft could have movable bases nearer their targets and could take off, land, and refuel without having to go all the way back to their home base on land. The U.S. carrier *Forrestal* is the largest warship driven by ordinary turbine engines. She can carry 90 to 100 planes and reach a speed of 34 knots. The largest warship in the world, however, is the American aircraft carrier *Enterprise*, which is run by atomic power.

Atomic power has also been put to use in other naval ships. Cruisers such as the American cruiser *Long Beach*, are atomic powered. The *Long Beach* carries guided missiles and can deal with any type of ship or aircraft armed with normal or atomic weapons. Modern atomic-powered submarines like the American *Nautilus* have helped to improve submarine warfare. *Nautilus* can move at 21 knots and can travel 40,000 sea miles before she needs more fuel. Britain's first atomic-powered submarine was the *Dreadnought*. It is clear that atomic power has constructive as well as destructive uses in modern warfare.

Until modern times, cargo ships mainly carried luxuries—spice, gold, silks, ivory, and other such things. Today we depend on shipping to carry the things we need to live—oil, grain, meat, timber, cotton, coal, steel, and many other materials.

Although cargo ships used to be rather ugly creatures, nowadays they are much more handsome and streamlined. There are two general types of cargo ships—tramps and cargo liners. The tramps do not have specific routes or special cargoes. They carry cargoes from port to port as needed, so that they may take grain to one port and there pick up a load of coal to carry on to the next. Cargo liners, on the other hand, carry cargoes on regular routes, and very often carry a small number of passengers as well. Many people enjoy the excitement of travel aboard a cargo ship where they can visit many different ports. It is also cheaper to travel this way than to book passage on an ocean liner.

More and more, however, cargo ships are being built specially to carry just one kind of material. In this way the ships may be designed to suit the cargo better and may be equipped with the best kind of unloading gear for the product the ship is handling. One good example of a special cargo ship is the oil tanker. Since oil is needed by people everywhere in the world, the modern oil tanker has to be able to carry lots of oil quickly from place to place. It has become one of the most advanced types of cargo vessel.

Because oil catches fire very easily, the engines and the funnel are well in the stern of the ship. This also means that the engines are near the ship's propellers so that the long shafts that connect the engines to the propellers do not have to go through the oil tanks. These ships may be un-

Coastal tankers are built smaller than ocean-going tankers so that they can get into ports that are too small and shallow for the big tankers. They sometimes take their cargoes right up rivers and canals.

loaded very quickly and spend less time in port than other cargo ships. To gain speed when the ship is at sea it pays to have as large a ship as possible, so tankers are getting bigger and bigger. Monster tankers like the 150,000-ton *Tokyo Maru* are being built. They are propelled by a single engine, which makes them among the most unusual ships afloat and because of their size, difficult to handle.

There are many other kinds of ships used in merchant shipping. Fishing trawlers, which drag large trawl nets behind them, are now being built so that they are like small factories. The fish are caught, made ready for selling and kept fresh—all on board so that the trawler may stay out fishing for as many as 80 days.

Another "factory ship" is a whaler like the *William Barendsz*. She has a crew of 500 men, 17 whale catchers, and 48 tanks for storing the whale oil. She provides so much oil that instead of coming back to port each time she has a full hold, other vessels have to go out and take some of the oil and whale meat from her and give her the supplies she needs.

Ferries are yet a third kind of merchant vessel. Simple river ferries are often paddle-driven and may be guided by a chain which is attached to either bank.

The timber carrier is specially built for its work. The cabins and pilothouse are all at one end, leaving a long deck onto which the lengths of timber are secured. Ships like this can carry wood from Norway all over Europe.

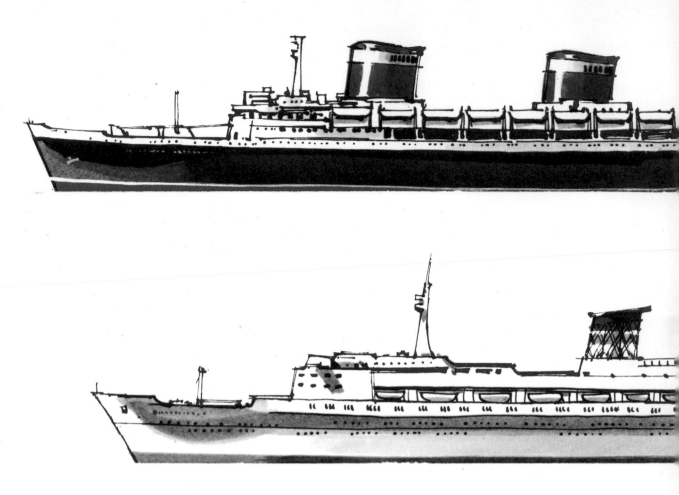

The ferry is also attached to the chain and runs up and down it. These small ferries can carry a few automobiles as well.

The ocean-going salvage tug is an interesting merchant ship, though it carries no cargo. These ships must stand ready at ports in all parts of the world to go to the rescue of vessels in distress. They are also used for towing old ships to the scrap yards, and for helping to salvage sunken ships. Recently, they have taken on a new job—that of towing oil and gas-drilling rigs into position to drill for oil under the sea.

From the day when the first real Atlantic passenger ship started making regular trips in 1871, ocean liners have rapidly become larger and more complicated. The first of these steamships had sails as well as engines, but by 1900 they ran on steam-power alone. As more and more ocean liners were built, a prize called the "Blue Riband" was begun, to be given to the liner that crossed the Atlantic the fastest. The *Mauretania*, launched in 1906, won the prize and was able to hold it for 22·years. In 1929 she was beaten by the German ship *Bremen*, which took the prize away from her.

In the 1930's Britain entered the contest for the Blue Riband with the launching of the *Queen Mary*. Her sister ship, the *Queen Elizabeth*, carried troops during

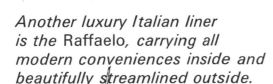

America entered the transatlantic race in 1952 with the United States, *which set two world speed records in that year.*

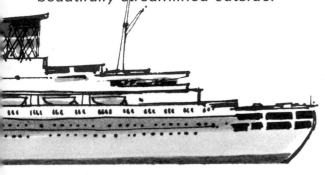

Another luxury Italian liner is the Raffaelo, *carrying all modern conveniences inside and beautifully streamlined outside.*

World War II and began to carry passengers after the war was over. The two ships ran regular trips until just recently. They have now both been retired, but the *Queen Mary* has been bought by an American who wants to keep it as a tourist attraction and the *Queen Elizabeth* has just been replaced by a new, modern *Queen Elizabeth II*.

The United States did not enter the transatlantic race until after World War II when the liner *United States* made her maiden voyage in 1952. The *United States*, though she is smaller than either of the two "Queens" is able to carry more passengers! She set two world speed records for transatlantic crossings in 1952.

Nowadays speed is not so important to liners as it was between the wars, since travellers who are in a hurry can travel by aeroplane. As a result ocean liners are designed to give passengers all the luxuries and comforts possible so that if people are not in a hurry to get somewhere they will prefer to travel by boat. One of these luxury liners is the *Rotterdam*, a Dutch ship that can carry 1,456 passengers. A special feature of the *Rotterdam* is special equipment that enables her to take the salt out of 700 tons of sea water a day and use the de-salted water instead of having to carry fresh water on board.

One of the most recent additions to the transatlantic fleets has come from Italy and is the *Leonardo da Vinci*, an ultra modern luxury liner that runs from Naples to New York in 7 days.

Another kind of large passenger ship is the "second-line ship", which cannot compete with the fastest liners and therefore must carry some cargo as well as passengers in order to stay in business. The *Coronia*, *America* and *Ile de France* are ships of this type, which take nearly twice as long to make the same trip that a ship like the *Rotterdam* makes. Still another kind of passenger ship is the cruise ship, designed for passengers who are not trying to get anywhere but merely want to enjoy a holiday on board a ship.

So far, atomic power has not been used to run passenger ships, but ship-builders are already thinking about this, and it will probably not be long before we will be able to cross the Atlantic on atomic-powered ocean liners.

The Solar System and the Stars

The sun, the centre of the solar system, is more than a million times the size of the earth. Its centre is very hot indeed—about 20,000,000 degrees C.—but its surface is only about 6,000 degrees C. The surface of the sun is very stormy; great uprushes of gas on its surface appear to us as sunspots.

The family of planets, including the earth, that make up our solar system, circle about the sun. Nine planets of considerable size are known, and their names in the order of their distances from the sun are: Mercury (closest), Venus, Earth, Mars, Jupiter, Saturn, Uranus, Neptune, Pluto. In addition, about 2,000 tiny planets, some of them only a few miles in diameter, swarm round the sun between Mars and Jupiter.

Mercury is about 36 million miles from the sun—less than half the distance of the earth from the sun. It is naturally much hotter than the earth, and is, in fact, far too hot for anything to live there.

Venus, 67 million miles from the sun, is also distinctly hotter than the earth, and is certainly too hot to support life. It has an atmosphere, too, but as this contains no oxygen we would not be able to breathe it.

Next after Venus comes the earth, which revolves about the sun at a distance of 93 million miles. The earth has one natural satellite—the moon, which revolves around it at a distance of only 240,000 miles. The moon always keeps the same side facing the earth, and it was not until the recent moon-probes that we were able to have photographs of the side facing away from the earth.

Mars, 142 million miles from the sun, is much smaller than the earth—only about one-quarter the size and one-tenth the weight—and it is certainly a colder planet. Though Mars has an atmosphere

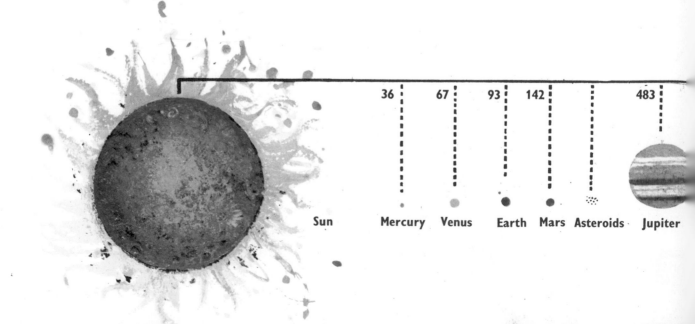

Sun   Mercury   Venus   Earth   Mars   Asteroids   Jupiter

36   67   93   142   483

In the last few years space scientists have been making close observations of the moon. Satellites, and more recently, a manned spacecraft, have been sent into orbit around it to record data and take photographs.

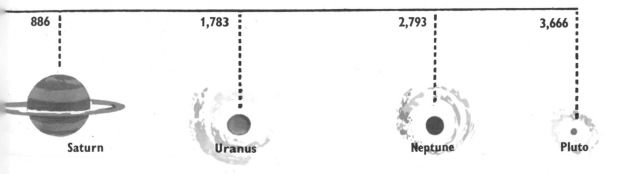

886 — Saturn

1,783 — Uranus

2,793 — Neptune

3,666 — Pluto

it contains no oxygen, and it is as thin as our own atmosphere at a height of 13 miles. There is water on Mars and the poles have snow-caps not unlike those in our own polar regions, though they are much thinner.

Nearly 500 million miles from the sun, spinning swiftly on its axis once every ten hours, is the giant planet Jupiter. Jupiter is larger than all the other planets put together and is equal to about 1,400 earths. It has an immense atmosphere, and vast belts of clouds completely surround the planet. Jupiter has twelve moons spinning around it.

Farther out still—so far that the sun itself now appears to be little more than a large star—is another giant planet, Saturn. Saturn is more than 800 times the size of the earth, but it is only 100 times as heavy. It is therefore a very light planet and would, in fact, float on water. It has nine moons, but its great glory is the system of three flat rings that encircle it at the equator. It is certain that these are not solid, but consist of swarms of particles—possibly ice-crystals.

Saturn is about 890 million miles from the sun, and beyond this there is nothing but empty space for another 900 million miles, when we come to the lonely planet Uranus. Uranus is so far from the sun that its "year"—the time it takes to go round the sun once—is equal to eighty-four of our years.

The next planet, Neptune, which circles the sun 1,000 million miles beyond Uranus, is very similar and has two moons. A thousand million miles beyond this planet lies Pluto, the outermost member of the sun's family. Pluto is a small planet and, like Uranus and Neptune, cannot be seen

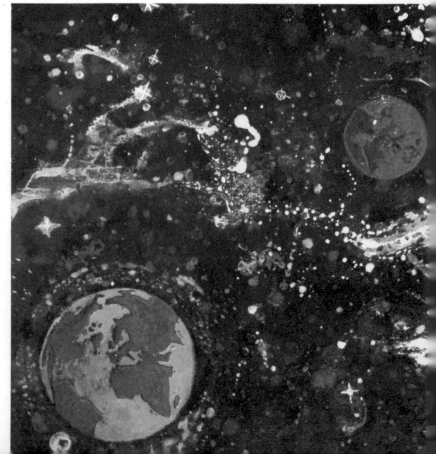

Every now and again, streams of flaming gases shoot miles into space from the sun's surface. These eruptions are known as solar prominences, and are perhaps the biggest danger to future space vehicles passing too near the sun—their heat would quickly turn such a craft into a cinder.

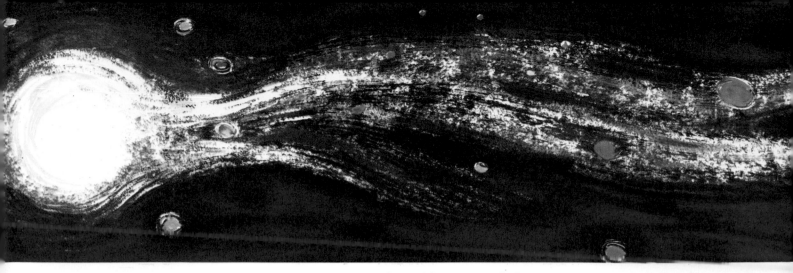

Comets are small heavenly bodies that move in orbits around the sun.
Halley's Comet, one of the most famous, passes the earth every 76 years.

without a telescope. Very little is known about it, though it must be very dark, intensely cold and quite unable to support life.

With the rapidly advancing space programmes of America and Russia our knowledge of the solar system, especially of the moon and the planets nearest the earth, will increase. Already we have close-up photographs of the moon, and a landing of astronauts on the actual surface of the moon is not far off.

Most of our great star-system—which we call the "Galaxy"—is hidden from us. In very recent years much of the hidden part of our Galaxy has been explored by means of radio-waves. Detecting these waves and mapping their directions has been one of the greatest achievements of the radio-telescopes.

Our Galaxy now appears to be rather different from the bun- or biscuit-shape it

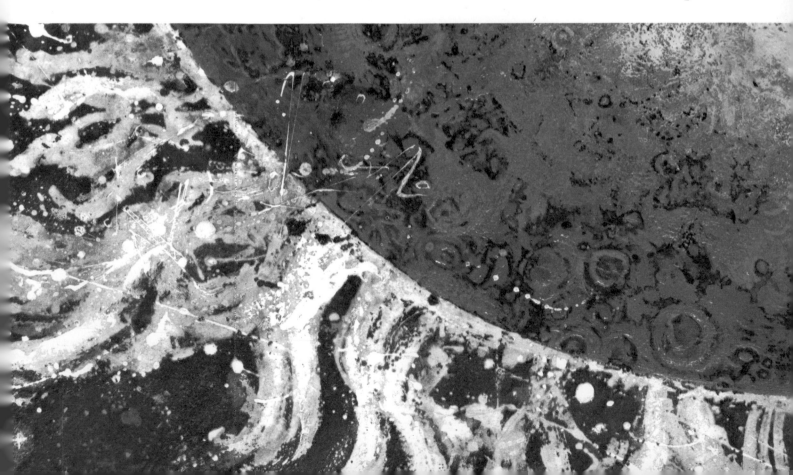

Above: *A spiral nebula very much the same shape as our own galactic system.* Below: *Artist's impression of the Universe, filled with numerous giant nebulae.*

was believed to have been. It is more like a Catherine-wheel. It spins round once every 200 million years, and it throws out three or four curved arms of gas and dust, all spangled with stars. The sun is just a small star towards the end of one of the arms, and it is travelling round the Galaxy at about 150 miles per second.

The clouds of dusty gas in our Galaxy can also sometimes be seen, and they are called "nebulae", the Latin word for clouds. Many of them are luminous, like the Great Nebula in Orion, which is just visible to the naked eye, but others are dark. Some of the dark ones can be seen as black silhouettes, when they happen to stand in front of a bright nebula or star cloud. The Horse's Head Nebula, also in Orion, is a good example. Nebulae form an important part of the Galaxy, for it is out of them

The Horse's Head Nebula in Orion gets its name from its distinctive shape.

that the stars themselves are born.

Since the discovery of our galaxy, many more such gigantic star-systems have been found, and altogether there must be thousands of millions of them. Because of their immense distances from each other, Sir William Herschel, an astronomer who lived in George III's reign, called them "island universes", but nowadays we generally call them "galaxies" (with a small "g").

We do not know how many "suns" with planets like the earth they may contain, and they are much too far away ever to be visited by any kind of spaceship. Even a super-spaceship could hardly visit the nearest star in our own Galaxy, which is 25 million million miles from the sun. Travelling at 186,000 miles per second, the trip would take 4 years, and the nearest island universe is 400,000 times as far off!

Space Travel

Even as recently as ten years ago, space travel was still largely a dream of rocket engineers. Now, however, it is a reality. Satellites and manned spacecraft have orbited the earth and, since December 1968, the moon. With the landing of astronauts on the moon and the gathering of more and more information about travelling in space, journeys to the planets may not be far off.

It is not possible to travel through empty space in aeroplanes or balloons because they require air to support them. For the purposes of leaving the earth's atmosphere and venturing into outer space, the rocket has been developed.

A rocket burns up all the fuel it can carry very quickly—often within two or three minutes of take-off. In order to get away from the earth it must reach a speed of about 7 miles per second before its fuel runs out. If it travels at only 4 miles per second it may go to a great height, but it will eventually fall back to earth again. If it travels at 5 miles per second it will go into a moon-like orbit around the earth. But at 7 miles per second it will escape the earth's gravitational pull altogether, so this speed is called the earth's "escape velocity". For heavier planets it would be much greater; for lighter ones, much less.

It has not so far been possible to build a rocket that can escape from the earth with a single effort. The method used is to build a rocket able to rise at 2 or 3 miles per second, and have it carry another, smaller rocket under its nose. When all of the first rocket's fuel is burnt out it automatically fires the second stage—the smaller rocket—and drops away. If necessary, a third stage rocket is provided to boost the craft farther into space.

In this way rockets have been sent to the moon and beyond the moon to such planets as Mars. As soon as they get clear of the earth, however, they come under the influence of the sun's gravitational pull. If they are travelling towards the

Opposite: *Space stations of the future will be permanent laboratories for scientific study.* Below: *Astronauts have successfully "walked" in space outside rocket capsules.* Right: *A three-stage rocket at take-off.*

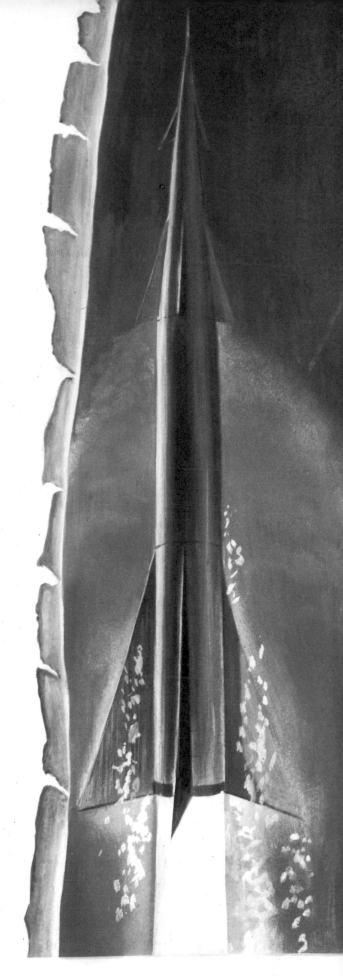

sun they will eventually fall into it, but otherwise they will orbit round it, like the planets. A number of them are doing so at this very moment.

One of the problems that still has to be solved if space flight is to become common will be to provide an artificial gravity system in the spaceship. Once the rocket is outside the earth's gravitational pull, it becomes weightless, and the men inside float about freely. The slightest movement of a man's foot on the floor will send him soaring to bump his head against the ceiling. If he stays quite still, he will gradually leave the floor and drift towards the centre of the cabin. If he tries to drink water from a glass he will find that the water refuses to pour out of the glass, which he can leave safely poised upside-down in the air.

Until this problem is solved, astronauts are working without gravity. They are generally strapped into their seats, and they eat special "space food", usually in liquid or tablet form, and have at hand various special devices that make life easier for them in their weightless state. A special shaver has even been designed for the astronauts' use which sucks up the shaved hairs like a vacuum-cleaner so that they do not float around the space capsule and clog up delicate instruments!

Then there is the problem of destination. If we want to visit Mars, for example, it will take two months at 7 miles per second to get there, for Mars is never less than 36 million miles from the earth. We should have to carry food and other essentials, not only for this period, but also for our stay on Mars and the return journey, when the earth and Mars would be several more million miles apart. We should also need breathing apparatus.

A journey to Mercury would take us too close to the sun, and parts of the space-craft would probably melt. Jupiter and Saturn have atmospheres that are poisonous to human beings and are so massive that if we landed on them, we should scarcely be able to move because of the increase in our weight. Also, their escape velocities are so high we should have no hope of ever getting away again. Visits to the stars would be out of the question, for it would take about 100,000 years to reach the nearest one.

Space flight will become much simpler when we discover how to use atomic energy for a rocket motor. One of the major difficulties with present-day rockets is the weight of the fuel that has to be carried. Chemical fuels, like liquid oxygen and gasoline, are carried by the ton and burned up at the rate of hundreds of gallons per second. But atomic energy—if we knew how to use it—would provide the same power for only a few ounces weight, and this would enable us to carry great reserves through space at the escape velocity. We might even travel at hundreds of miles per second. This would bring the entire solar system within range, but it would still take 100 years to reach the nearest star even if we travelled at the fantastic speed of 10,000 miles per second. Atomic energy, however, has its own special drawbacks. It releases dangerous radiations and it might be necessary to weigh down the spaceship with heavy lead shields to protect the passengers. Firing the rocket, too, would probably drench the launching site with radioactive matter and poison the earth's atmosphere. All the same, these difficulties may one day be overcome, and space flight may become as common as air travel is today.

Artist's impression of a space vehicle for inter-planetary travel in the not-too-distant future. At bottom right is a space station, a stopping-point for these vehicles where they may put in for supplies and more fuel for the long journey ahead.

Things We Eat

When primitive man felt the pangs of hunger he simply went hunting, or ate the wild fruits and berries he found growing nearby. Even cooking was unknown to him before the discovery of fire, and he ate his meat raw. Nowadays, however, the many different kinds of food we know and the various methods we have of preparing them make the subject of food a much more complicated one and one which has a long history of its own.

The people of the Middle Stone Age were the first to discover how to sow seeds and produce crops. That seeds sprout and grow into plants must have been noticed many times before this, but the idea of gathering seeds and sowing them on a plot of ground, and then waiting for the plants to come up, was something quite new. This was really an invention—not a "discovery"—and it was the invention of farming.

The practice of farming spread far and wide during the next few thousand years. In the mild climate of western Asia and northern Africa the fertile mud on the banks of the rivers Euphrates and Tigris, the Jordan and the Nile, was found capable

One of man's favourite fruits is the peach. Peach trees grow well in the warmer areas of the world and produce fruits with a smooth, juicy flesh. True peaches have a fuzzy outer skin, while the nectarine, another variety of peach, has a very smooth skin.

A bird's-eye-view of a new method of cultivating the land to increase crop yield on a farm in the state of Washington, in America.

of growing crop after crop, and men began to settle down in small towns surrounded by the first permanent farms.

Cereals have been grown by man from the very earliest times; in fact, there was no other group of plants more important to man's rise to civilization. Many excavations made in Egypt, Mexico and Peru have revealed primitive store places or granaries for harvested grain. So important were the crops that most of these early people gave gifts of cereals to their gods, and sometimes left small pots of grain in the graves of people who had died. This was done to ensure that the departed would have something to eat on their way to the next life. Among the gods worshipped by the ancient Romans was Ceres, who was thought to be the guardian of the grain crops and harvest. It is from the goddess Ceres that we get the name cereal.

All cereals can be traced back to wild grasses. It is by man's cultivation and selection over thousands of years that we

151

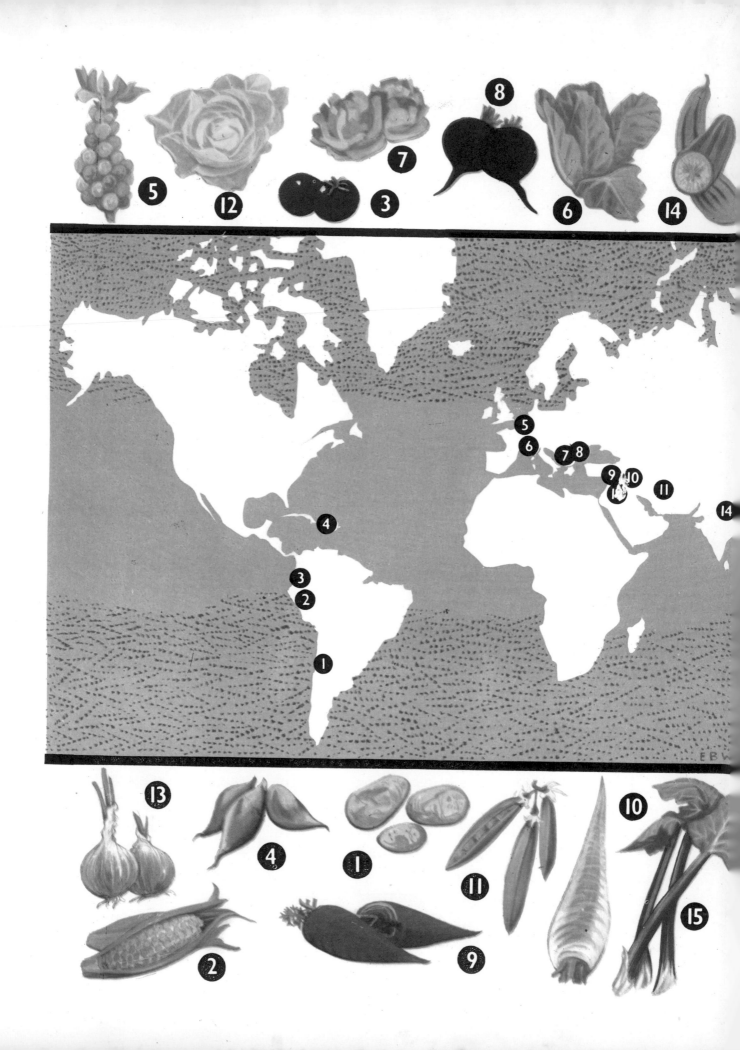

To find out which parts of the world the vegetables pictured here originally came from, match the number beside each vegetable with the number that is marked on the map.

now have a wide variety of cereals. They provide the basis of our food whether directly eaten, as in the form of rice, breakfast cereals, bread, cakes, biscuits, etc. or indirectly as food for the animals which we eat in the form of meat, milk, eggs and butter.

In the last hundred years the world has grown tremendous quantities of cereals to keep pace with the growing population. By far the most important cereals are wheat, rice and maize. Other cereals are barley, oats, rye, sorghum and millet.

As farming became more and more widespread, new crops such as peas, beans, and flax (for making linen and linseed oil) were added to the cereals. Sheep and goats were caught and tamed. Later, wild pigs and cattle found prowling around homesteads at night were added to the farm stock; these were the first domestic animals. Nowadays the raising of animals such as cattle, sheep and pigs is done on a very large scale in some countries, and meat is an important export product of such countries as Australia, New Zealand, Argentina, Canada and the United States.

At some point in the early days of farming, someone planted the first apple orchard. Today the cultivation of fruit, too, is a large-scale industry, and with speedy means of transport and refrigerated carriers we can now enjoy fresh fruits that are not grown in our own areas. The apples, pears, cherries, peaches and plums that grow in the temperate areas of the world can be served side by side with semi-tropical or tropical fruits such as oranges, lemons, bananas and pineapples.

1	potatoes	8	red beetroots
2	maize	9	carrots
3	tomatoes	10	parsnip
4	sweet potatoes	11	peas
5	Brussels sprouts	12	lettuce
6	cabbage	13	onions
7	globe artichokes	14	cucumbers
		15	rhubarb

153

Farming today is the world's largest industry, and is likely to remain so because of the world's rapidly increasing population. In the main, especially in Britain and America, the farmer is no longer content to use the old traditional ways of farming, but draws on science and engineering to help him out. Some modern farms are now completely mechanised, so much so that it is becoming a rare sight to see a horse doing a farm job. Further, man is looking for new areas of farming and already experiments are going on to see how in the future man can farm the sea for fish and other forms of sea life. In Japan and China, in fact, seaweed has for centuries been an important "crop"; harvesting weed from the coasts and islands around Japan is now a big industry.

We tend to think that the vegetables we know so well today have always been with us. Yet as late as Elizabethan times very few of the vegetables that now grow in such abundance were widely cultivated. When the tomato was brought into European gardens from South America in the 16th century, it was grown for decoration long before people began to eat it. Other vegetables, like the potato, were considered scarcely fit to eat.

All vegetables are derived from plants originating in widely scattered parts of the world. Botanists today can say where and when most of our vegetables were first grown, but some spread through wide areas so long ago that it is impossible to give exact dates. We know that the garden pea is at least as old as the pyramids of Egypt. The lettuce, onion, and leek are also likely to have been cultivated since

Planting out rice in a paddy field in Madagascar, now the Malagasy Republic. Rice is the staple diet on which millions of people in Africa and Asia subsist.

Herring

Salmon

Cod

Plaice

Skate

Left: *Some varieties of ocean fish that are commonly considered to be good eating.* Below: *Although England is a densely populated and industrial country, she must preserve her rich agricultural land for the production of the food she needs.*

prehistoric times. Beetroot was known to the Greeks long before the birth of Christ, but rhubarb has the oldest recorded history of all. It is recorded in ancient documents as having been used as medicine in China—the home of its origin—as long ago as 2700 B.C. Most of the varieties of cucumber grown today were known and cultivated throughout Europe at least 400 years ago. They originated from plants growing in the part of India that lies to the south-east of the Himalayan range. Globe artichokes also first became a delicacy in the ancient world, while the Jerusalem artichoke, a different vegetable altogether, is a native of the North American Continent, and did not appear in Europe until the 17th century.

155

Where People Live

If someone from outer space were to ask you to tell him where people on our planet live and what a house looks like, you would have to tell him about many different kinds of houses, for all over the world people have different ideas of what a house is and what it should be made of. Wherever men have built shelters for themselves, they have built them with the materials available and to suit the climate in which they live.

Most people live in groups, whether they are in the tiniest village of only three or four families or in a bustling city with millions of others. This, too, makes a difference in the kinds of houses people live in, for though people in smaller towns or in the country have enough room to build individual houses for themselves, city people often have to live in enormous blocks of flats which may house several hundred families.

In hot, dry climates where few trees grow and the soil is sandy, many people build their homes out of clay and mud. They make bricks which dry hard in the sun, and build low, flat-roofed houses that are cool inside even in the hottest weather.

A village of small, sun-baked huts in the Punjab, a part of India. People in villages like this one grow mostly cereal crops and vegetables on the flat, dry plains around their homes.

In this picture the artist shows how villages, towns and cities work together to bring people the things they need. Fishing villages and farms provide food, towns and cities manufacture goods and handle trade, and capital cities are centres of government and banking.

A village of thatched houses. Grasses are used for building in most of the Pacific Islands.

The Indians of the south-western United States and some Mexicans live in houses of this type, which are built of sun-dried clay, or *adobe*. If you go to other areas of the world that have the same type of dry, hot climate, such as parts of India, Africa, and the Middle East, you will find that people live in houses very much like the adobe houses of the Americas.

A different kind of hot-weather house is common in regions where there is more rainfall and therefore more trees and grasses about. These are the grass huts and houses lived in by people in Africa,

Blocks of modern flats and offices in Rio de Janeiro, a modern city in Brazil.

Asia and the South Pacific islands. The thick roofs of woven grasses on these houses help to keep out the hot sun. Naturally grass houses do not look exactly alike in all parts of the world, since they have been built by different people with different ideas about what a house should be. At the same time, however, it is remarkable that houses in such completely different parts of the world, built by people of different races and cultures, should be as alike as they are.

The same holds true for the nomadic, or wandering peoples of the world. These people do not have permanent homes but move about from place to place as they search for fresh pasture for their flocks of sheep and cattle. They very often live in tents, which they can pack up easily and carry with them wherever they go. Whether they are desert nomads of North Africa or wandering sheep herders in Central Asia they have found that tents are the best type of shelter for their kind of life.

Where many people come to live and work together, a town or city develops. There are many different kinds of towns and many reasons for their existence. In coastal areas, the places where there are natural harbours for ships are often the sites of towns or cities, for wherever ships dock, lots of trading and business is carried on. Other towns have grown up where there are large universities—Oxford and Cambridge in England are good examples of this. The people in these towns rely very much for their living on the people who come to the university to teach or to learn. Manufacturing towns usually arise where

The desert nomads of North Africa who live in tents like this one depend on the camel for almost everything they need. Camels not only supply them with a means of travel, but with food, clothing and shelter as well.

the raw materials for their manufacturers are to be found. Coal and iron towns naturally grow up where there are deposits of coal and iron ore. Kalgoorlie, on the edge of the Great Victoria Desert in Australia, grew up around the camps of the gold prospectors, as did Klondike, in Alaska. There are towns like Simla, in India, that have grown simply because the climate of the region around them is healthy, or because the local springs contain water of medicinal value. Towns supplying medicinal waters are called "spas", after the town of Spa in Belgium.

The word "city" in English means the same as "town", but we usually use "city" to refer to an old or very large town, or one to which the government of a large area of the country has been entrusted. The city which is chosen as the centre of government for the whole country is called its "capital", a word which simply means "head". A capital city will therefore contain important government buildings, and all the people who work in the government offices will live in or near the city.

ACKNOWLEDGMENTS

The publisher wishes to thank the following for supplying the excellent photographs which illustrate this work: Afrique Photo/Demesse 159; Afrique Photo/Langlais 154; Afrique Photo/Naud 10; Afrique Photo/Vincent 11; Air France 4; Atlas Photos 47, 89; Australian News and Information Bureau 23; Bordas 51; Collin-Delavaud 12, 13, 14, 87; P. Dempster 23, 24, 48, 157; Dupaquier 42, 46, 47, 48, 155; Goldner 17, 86; Henrard 49; Hétier 17; Idoux 8; Laferrere 15; Colette Landy 42; Le Brec 88, 112; Le Lannou 49, 50, 52; Lockwood Survey Corp. 19; Ozello 15, 17; Alain Perceval 50; B. Pierre 11; Marc Riboud/Magnum 88; Robillard 13, 86, 90, 158; A. A. Shipton 16; Stevens 43; Suinot 112, 115; Haroun Tazieff 8, 22, 45; U.S.I.S. 18, 113, 151; United States Travel Service 16; Vasselet 9; Villeminot 24; Wagner 43.

Index